SCENE CHANGE 3

The Ones Who Get It

What People Are Saying About

Scene Change 3: The Ones Who Get It

Alan Harrison is back with more tough love for the nonprofit arts sector. Alan challenges all of us to be laser-focused on putting community impact first. If you're looking for help in re-centering your organization on lifting people up through the arts, this book offers advice and case studies that will inspire you and help you get ready for the hard work ahead. Alan's perspective on the field is an important one to consider in order to expand the base of support for the arts.
Hannah Grannemann, Assistant Professor and Director of the Arts Administration Program, University of North Carolina at Greensboro

Wonderful! My students get sound business information from our standard textbook, but they get genuine, hard knocks wisdom from all the *Scene Change* books. They cut to the chase and challenge them to think practically and meaningfully. We do an exercise where they write a "standard" Mission Statement and an "Alan Harrison" Mission Statement – it knocks the empty, lofty rhetoric out of their statements and gets them to the heart of the matter. I also really value Alan Harrison's no-nonsense emphasis on genuinely serving the community.
Elizabeth Carlin Metz, Smith V. Brand Distinguished Professor of Theatre; Chair, Department of Theatre; and Director, Program in Arts Administration, Knox College | Founding Artistic Director, Vitalist Theatre, Chicago

Rave Reviews For

Scene Change and *Scene Change 2*

Game-changing! Pulls no punches! Many in the nonprofit arts sector will decry this manifesto as heresy, only validating its necessity. Drawing on his 30 years of experience in nonprofit theater, the author breaks down, in easy-to-understand language, the United States tax code and the ways in which nonprofit groups misconstrue their responsibilities as a 501(C)(3): "The purpose of nonprofit arts organizations is not about the production of art, but the production of impact using the arts as tools." Harrison also discusses the toxic influences within these organizations, including the lie of subscription revenue, glory-chasing artistic directors, and overly pampered big-money donors. The author proposes pragmatic reforms placing focus on better outreach to the neighborhoods these organizations operate in. Better diversity, equity, and inclusion (DEI) integration both on the boards and staffs, along with transparency regarding both donations and pay, would increase hospitality and impact, per Harrison. He argues that fostering diverse voices would help institutions to better understand the specific issues that require a nonprofit's help — be that aiding the houseless, combating gun violence, or raising awareness about the opioid crisis — while putting on shows that both engage and matter to the community. While forceful, even the harshest commentary is not presented prescriptively, and it clearly comes from a place of love for the subversive and utopian possibilities of the arts.
Kirkus Reviews, [*Scene Change*]

A truly gifted writer! In his brilliantly unpretentious, snarky, and hilarious style, Alan Harrison pulls no punches. He

identifies and addresses elitism, defines and defuses toxicity, and provides outlines for success, including a hopeful prediction for the future.
Anne Carlini, *Exclusive Magazine* [*Scene Change*]

It's very funny! Frankly, I didn't know what to expect. It's very funny — that was one of the biggest things I was struck by. It feels like Alan is talking to me in a normal, congenial way, rather than a dry arts management textbook-type thing. We have enough of those ... So fun!
Katie Birenboim, *Call Time* [*Scene Change*]

Comprehensive! Harrison contends that the organizational structure of nonprofit boards should be reexamined and notes that leadership strategies that may have worked in the 1970s aren't viable today. He has an easy, engaging style and provides a usable blueprint for how to start, reconfigure, and run a board. "Harrison's Rules of Order" covers how to conduct efficient meetings and outlines six rules (e.g., "Don't waste the money you've budgeted for board meetings by talking about items that you cannot change") that will help any arts board meeting — and other boards, as well — run more smoothly. Also included are exercises for boards to tackle together, which are sometimes based on real-life situations. This is a great starting point for any organization looking to run more smoothly.
Kirkus Reviews [*Scene Change 2*]

First Books in This Series

Scene Change:
Why Today's Nonprofit Arts Organizations
Have to Stop Producing Art and Start Producing Impact
ISBN 978-1803414461

Scene Change 2:
The Five ***Real*** *Responsibilities of*
Nonprofit Arts Boards
ISBN 978-1803416984

Every impactful 501(C)(3), including nonprofit arts organizations, is an experiment in making a better world. The chain of events in this experiment generally have to follow this formula:

1. Use your powers as a charitable organization to prove worth.
2. Quantifiable proof of worth provides funding.
3. Funding pays for programs.
4. Programs mitigate or eliminate your community's problems.
5. The mitigation or elimination of a community's problems extols equity, lessens hardships, provides safety and security, and overall, produces a better community.

Lather, rinse, repeat.

Or, of course, you could always choose to run a commercial arts venture. There's no moral high ground to running a nonprofit arts organization.

SCENE CHANGE 3

The Ones Who Get It

Alan Harrison

Edited by Michelle Auerbach

CHANGEMAKERS
BOOKS

London, UK
Washington, DC, USA

CollectiveInk

First published by Changemakers Books, 2025
Changemakers Books is an imprint of Collective Ink Ltd.,
Unit 11, Shepperton House, 89 Shepperton Road, London, N1 3DF
office@collectiveinkbooks.com
www.collectiveinkbooks.com
www.changemakers-books.com

For distributor details and how to order please visit the 'Ordering' section on our website.

ISBN: 978 1 80341 977 0
978 1 80341 728 8 (ebook)
Library of Congress Control Number: 2024948937

A CIP catalogue record for this book is available from the British Library.

Design: Lapiz Digital Services

UK: Printed and bound by CPI Group (UK) Ltd, Croydon, CR0 4YY
Printed in North America by CPI GPS partners

We operate a distinctive and ethical publishing philosophy in all areas of our business, from our global network of authors to production and worldwide distribution.

Contents

Introduction — But Hey, Read It Anyway

First, a pre-introduction.

The most important thing to remember about any book I've written: write in it yourself (unless you've picked this up in a public library, of course). Dog-ear the pages. Write notes to yourself. Flesh out ideas as they apply to you. Mark up passages that speak to you. Mark up passages that speak against you. Use a pen, or if you're reading this electronically, highlight to your heart's content. This book is for you to use, not to admire (although admiration is a lovely thing). Go nuts. If you need an unvarnished copy for a friend to mark up, just buy another one. It's cheaper than therapy and less painful than banging your head against a stage apron in the Sisyphean agony that working with a nonprofit arts organization too often triggers.

Got your pen ready? Figured out the highlighter doohickey on your Kindle? Good. Now to the introduction.

There's a ginormous number 3 in big bold type on the cover of this book. The number 3 is not for show or to celebrate some quasi-religious trilogy.

So, if you haven't guessed, this is the third book in the series. It will probably be the last book in this series because, well, I said so. If you have not read the first two books, stop reading this book now and buy them. Or get them out of the library. Or borrow copies from the friend who told you to buy this book. Just don't steal them. But somehow, get them.

Then read them.

Then return to this point of the preface after consuming them. Don't worry — they're neither long nor laborious, and you might get a chuckle here and there. If you are, were, or want to be a leader for a nonprofit arts organization, the information contained in those two books is of paramount importance to your success. I may be breezy and all, but that last part's true as hell.

When you come back, I'll be right here. Just look for the picture of a panda as a bookmark. It's not a meaningful image. I just like pandas.

If you are at this point in the book, you have either already read the first two books or you've *just finished* those selfsame books and found the panda. Good job.

Or, conversely, you're Phil.

Phil's been doing this arts thing a long time and doesn't have the capacity to change. He doesn't even see the need. Phil is only reading this because someone told him to read it. With resolute stubbornness, Phil refused to read the first two books because this is America, people have the right to be as puddin'-headed as they choose, and because he is certain he knows more than I do. All of which might be true (not really, but we'll let Phil enjoy his fantasies).

Now, to recap the series (not for you, mind you, but for others who may have forgotten what they were about), in *Scene Change: Why Today's Nonprofit Arts Organizations Have to Stop Producing Art and Start Producing Impact,* we laid out the series of problems that plague the nonprofit arts organization world. We talked about elitism, DEI, and the manifest belief system that has driven arts organizations beyond the brink to full-on closure. While we discussed the COVID lockdown years of 2020–2022, we concluded that all the pandemic served to do was to rush organizations to shut down just a little quicker. Then, we concluded that there is a path to success for nonprofit arts organizations; it's just not the path on which they currently perambulate.

The biggest problem, of course, is that too many nonprofit arts organizations refuse to accept their charitable status except as it may be used to attract donors. That leads to a system where donors donate so that they may attend. When the donor becomes the beneficiary of the donation (something only nonprofit *arts* organizations do, while the rest of the nonprofit sector looks on in disgust), it begets toxicity among donors, executives, and board leadership, and provides an elitist barrier to participants.

That problem leads to bad behavior among organizations desperate to survive crappy management without actually changing the way in which they do business. Those are the folks that do things like emergency funding campaigns whereby they put a figurative .357 Magnum to their own head and threaten to pull the trigger unless they get a cash bailout. Kinda like the scene in *Blazing Saddles* where Cleavon Little points his gun at his own neck. If the emergency campaign somehow succeeds (or if a mysterious donation comes in to take them over the top), they continue to do all the things they did before, somehow believing that the result will be any different. They blow their chance to find the real purpose, their most charitable reason for being.

Ticket-buying is a commercial activity. While many businesses look at their revenue streams and see success when money is rolling in, nonprofits are supposed to look at their revenue streams and see success when the intended charitable impact (you know, those things in Section 501(C)(3) of the Internal Revenue Service code, which Phil hasn't bothered to read) comes to pass. Currently, most nonprofit arts organizations evaluate their revenue streams and plead that "Only 50% of our income comes from ticket sales, so please give." A true nonprofit would be better off considering an approach that says that "Only 50% of our income comes from donations; to do the real work, we also have to sell tickets." But they don't. Because they're still running nonprofit arts organizations as though they were for-profit, commercial entities, where ticket revenue is king.

Diversity/Equity/Income (DEI) has become a performative, do-nothing program rooted in the idea of having those in the Global Majority (non-Whites) act in their own best interests. They continue to decide how nonprofit arts organizations are to act. It was White people who believed that something as banal as "color-blind" casting was a revolutionary action (it's not). White-led boards tried to diversify their board membership by getting a few Black or Latino people to serve alongside them, as long as nothing much changed in the way in which the company does business. Can't frighten away the elitists, the White moderate folks who Dr. Martin Luther King described so eloquently in a letter from a Birmingham jail cell in 1963:

> I must make two honest confessions to you, my Christian and Jewish brothers. First, I must confess that over the past few years I have been gravely disappointed with the white moderate. I have almost reached the regrettable conclusion that the Negro's great stumbling block in his stride toward freedom is not the White Citizen's Counciler [*sic*] or the Ku Klux Klanner, but the white moderate, who is more devoted to 'order' than to justice; who prefers a negative peace which is the absence of tension to a positive peace which is the presence of justice; who constantly says: 'I agree with you in the goal you seek, but I cannot agree with your methods of direct action'; who paternalistically believes he can set the timetable for

> another man's freedom; who lives by a mythical concept of time and who constantly advises the Negro to wait for a 'more convenient season.' Shallow understanding from people of good will is more frustrating than absolute misunderstanding from people of ill will. Lukewarm acceptance is much more bewildering than outright rejection.

Rather than affecting the most change in order to increase cultural celebration and charitable impact, most (especially large) nonprofit arts organizations seek to eke out the least change they can in order to keep familiar, ineffective practices going. They see DEI programs as just another distraction from their life's calling to produce more of the same. When it costs money to enact, they jettison DEI more quickly than a fiery wad of ghost pepper chewing gum.

We discussed that ageism is rampant among nonprofit arts organizations, which is a ridiculous waste of talent. Lifespans are not getting longer — people are not suddenly living 120 years or more — but, with more emphasis on health, diet, exercise, and the better availability of the medical system in America (unless you're a woman, of course, because, evidently, the plight of your body belongs to the Supreme Court) more people are living to a maximized lifespan (80–100) with greater mental acuity. All that being said, nonprofit arts organizations that have hired experienced workers over the age of 50 into full-time, non-executive roles are as rare as goose-down anoraks in Tegucigalpa. There's a lot of active brain and experiential power between the ages of 50 and 70 and later. All that is part of DEI, too.

We talked about the difference among art, artists, and arts organizations. These are three different things, not one. To summarize, *art* is essential in the literal sense (like air or water) because there is no environment in which art does not already exist, both natural and man-made. *Artists* are magical because they can take disparate things, combine them, and create a new art with its own value. *Nonprofit arts organizations* are not essential at all because art and artists can (and do) exist without them, they do not create art but rather produce or present it, and their nonprofit status seems not to compel them to do any charitable work that interferes with their main function, which is to, um, well, that's hard to say.

"Art for art's sake" is a crock as a mission for arts organizations; as a friend of mine put it, "If art is for art's sake, then let Art pay for it." Phil and his kind always seem to fall back on the specious "art for art's sake" argument.

The whole purpose of a food bank is not to show how shiny the shelves are or how fresh the produce is. It's to find ways to feed people who need it. Similarly, arts organizations have fallen into the trap of believing that the art they produce is somehow enough to justify their charitable status. It's not.

No, Phil, it's not.

We talked about various other things like the Irony-Free Police and the destructive legacy of cancel culture, the story of *The Tortoise and the Hare and the Ants,* and the role mischief has to play in building a better arts-mosphere. Gotta read the first book to get those references. Which, if you're not Phil, you've already done.

Finally, we talked about the wonders available in a new world based on the cyclical nature of humanity in America. We talked about the tiresome nature of dystopian futures and the point at which a new, better future can be built from the rubble of the current field of artists. We talked about steps you can take to make your nonprofit arts organization create the kind of world you want to live in — the kind of world that might even make a better world for your kids.

In *Scene Change 2: The Five Real Responsibilities of Nonprofit Arts Boards,* we created a set of exercises, ideas, talking points, and debate questions on how to make a board of directors that can support an exciting future instead of a droning past. The framework of a successful board in 2025 and beyond will have to be constructed of people who care more about impact than about *Robert's Rules of Order*, zealots who understand that democracy and consensus are two completely different things (you want consensus-driven decision making, not democracy), and that most of the rules that have been set up for board governance actually work against the idea of creating the kind of impact that makes your community a better place to live.

We talked about organizational charts and who actually owns the business (no, it's not the board — but that's close). We talked about the downside of artistic directorships and the upside of executive directorships, given that in all other kinds of nonprofit organizations, the executive director is the person most responsible for ensuring mission execution.

There was a lot of chatter about these books. A lot of hate mail from those whose lives have been challenged. A lot of pushback from those who believe that — and on some level, I find this shocking coming from supposedly knowledgeable and experienced businesspeople, some of whom I've trusted for years — somehow, arts organizations are not "nonprofit," and are certainly not "charities," but instead are something called "non-commercial."

As we all know, "non-commercial" is not a phrase in the law, nor does it appear in the IRS code governing what activities are acceptable for nonprofit organizations, nor is it anything but a euphemism for those who believe that performing charity is beneath them. It's a term from elitists to describe their work so that they still reap donations while not admitting that the organization itself is not centered on work that is charitable. A terrible two-step of disingenuousness hidden behind a word that, while true in a lower-case sense, has no official meaning for 501(C)(3) corporations.

It's as though, as an arts organization, some companies do not want to be forced into helping those who need it. They only want to be responsible to entertain those that donate to it. Somehow, these associates from years past are *defending* that idea, which is evil, desperate, and a flat-out fraudulent lie.

In that vein, a good friend and a fan of the books recently wrote to me. "You are pushing upstream," she warned, "against an entire industry that wants to call minuscule iteration a 'tectonic shift.' Even DEI has become a feeding trough exploited by folks who want to 'get theirs.' People are paranoid and terrified that their livelihoods are going to be taken away by the economy and by calls for change ... Frankly, I think many of these people have never been challenged and are terrified they cannot keep up."

Pushing upstream is tiring. One doesn't choose to swim upstream unless one is caught in a riptide, undertow, or a deadly current that inevitably leads to, say, a fatal waterfall. Swimming upstream is neither profitable nor all that popular, at least in my experience. It has forced me to change jobs — sometimes my doing, sometimes the company's doing — more than once. But, I know my own conscience, I know the difference between right and wrong when it comes to nonprofit impact, and I know that there is a better path. I'm not saying I've been a perfect leader. I have most certainly *not*. I've fallen into the same traps as every other arts leader. And more. I'm just saying that the organizations in this book have as close to perfect leadership as one could hope for. And none of those leaders are named "Phil."

I never wrote these books to make money. I just want people to know how to fix the problem. I suppose I underestimated just how many egos (and, presumably, livelihoods) are tied to continuing elitism issues in the nonprofit arts.

I've written this trilogy for two audiences. The first is comprised of the leaders who have become tired of producing art for the wrong reasons — among them vainglory, peer acclaim, résumé building, and strictly personal satisfaction. I wrote the book for the leaders who want to find a path toward a terrific future for their communities. People who float from job to job, from city to city — as I myself had done in the past — are participants in a system that rewards childlessness, independent wealth, and 168-hour weekly availability among its leaders.

The second audience is me, or rather the 30-year-old version of me that became a department head for the first time. There are lots of people in that stage of leadership right now. For you, this series might lead to great things. Certainly arguments with the old guard, which is never bad. After all, it's how they got to their leadership positions, too. But more than that, you can point to the lessons and ideas in these books as you argue for the better, impactful path for your own nonprofit arts organization.

Worker exploitation — the aforementioned 168-hour weeks, for example, because the toxic peer pressure of working for free has become so prevalent — is not a problem limited to arts organizations. The pandemic shutdown proved that family time is more important than work time. Abusive jobs and caustic workplaces where employees are asked to donate 20 hours or more per week back to the company — and don't even get a tax break for doing so — have become anathema to most Americans.

Companies have been trained to drain every last drop out of their workers in order to serve the shareholders. Is that the kind of nonprofit arts industry you want?

Scene Change 3 takes a completely different tack than the first two in the series (although, again, it will make far more sense if you've read the first two, especially in a workgroup, book group, or classroom setting for *Scene Change 2*). In this book, I'll talk about the characteristics of a great nonprofit arts organization in Chapter 1. As the third book in a trilogy, I felt that it was important to let you know that there are, in fact, organizations that, after drifting around as companies that never quite found fulfillment or excellence in their regions, made the change to center their community's needs over their own and succeeded as charities because of that decision. There are organizations who choose to serve the public and measure their impact not in the decrepit ways of the butts-in-seats, economic impact, or national test-score data (all of which are useless as metrics), but in the aspects of their own community that become healthier by the work they do.

In this book we'll uncover nonprofit arts organizations that have saved people's lives. Literally. As in, some people would be dead without their intervention. In this process, I studied the organizations for about a year and embedded in their operations for a month each. I went to work with them, sat in on meetings (including board meetings), experienced the art as many times and in as many ways as I could do, met with local political officials and other arts leaders in their communities (to get a sense of the "arts-mosphere," a new word I've just coined) of the city, state, and region. In addition, I interviewed as many audience participants as humanly possible, wherever they happened to be, painstakingly transcribing each interview. In order to understand the success of the organization and that relationship to their collective decision to refuse to act like every other arts organization within their discipline, it was important to me to see whether the success was fluky or real.

In all cases contained herein, I'm convinced the success is real, the impact is real, and the intent — to make their communities better utilizing art not as a product, but as a tool — drives them to their goals. These organizations are well-run, zealous in their mission as a charitable organization, and winning where other arts organizations are losing.

When we discuss the stakes of other nonprofit arts organizations *vis-à-vis* the ones in this book, we cannot let the discussion begin and end with the participants or the inner workings. If the goal is hollow, then the results are irrelevant.

It matters if the community is better off in measurable ways because of an arts organization. *That's* the risk in embarking on the journey of running one. So, when you hear your next artistic director or columnist or board chair brag about "the risk-taking programming," you'll know that you need to dismiss that twaddle with a grain of NaCl. Risk-taking is not casting Billy Porter as Billy Bigelow in *Carousel*. That's just eye-rolling puffery for no reason whatsoever except to engage in weird self-aggrandizement for a vainglorious artistic director.

I've heard amazing people talk about the power of the art to change minds without causing harm. That's not enough.

It's not enough "not to cause harm." It's not enough to strive to change a mind (or *strive* to do anything, really) without that change resulting in positive transformation for the community that owns your company. It's not enough to present beauty and culture and harmony without lasting impact. It's not enough to do the latest play or the most difficult opera or the most athletic dance choreography if you're doing it for applause and ticket sales. That's no different than Disney selling tickets to theme parks for hundreds of dollars apiece. Or libraries that believe that literacy is solved by the paper, cardboard, and glue that comprise unread books. It's not enough.

So when I use the phrase "the ones who get it," I'm talking about organizations who understand what it means to be a nonprofit. They value the charitable aspect of what they do because they saw a problem and tried to solve it. They decided there were enough theaters in America. Enough orchestras in America. Enough arts organizations of all kinds in America — at last count 133,000 of them that have 501(C)(3) letters. What there weren't — before they began doing their work in their communities — were organizations whose missions could only be done by them. They saw that art could be used as a vibrant tool for the underserved, rather than as a nifty distraction for the privileged. Not only did that turn their focus outward, they received moral and financial stability by virtue of their charitable works and results.

Visit these organizations. Donate to them. Read about them as they flourish and know that you can help them help their communities be better places in which to live. To people running arts organizations across America, learning how and why they succeed is easy. All you have to do is bring humility to the table and, rather than argue for your way of doing business (which may help nobody but you), absorb why these companies succeed in helping, educating, and getting social commitments from the people they touch. Wanting to do community service in lieu of what you're currently doing — ay, there's the rub.

Phil, you might become uncomfortable with what crosses your mind while reading this series. That's good. An editor (who hired me for a project after saying this) once told me that my writing was "annoyingly compelling." My goal here is to let you know that your nonprofit arts organization needn't be welded to an artistic vision, performance-driven beauty, or some undefinable term such as "artistic excellence" in order to be successful. In fact, it's more likely to become successful when you can throw all that ostentatious detritus in the scrap heap of lexicography. It may oblige you to change your organizational thinking for the better. Or it may cause you to retire. I'm good either way. We all are.

As for those of you who are not Phil, whether you're an executive, an artist, a staff member, a board member, an audience member, a donor, a government official, or a mother of four living in your car, the arts can help your community make better choices. It can be done. Only the most stubborn, me-first, art-for-art's-sake megalomaniacs create a charity that only benefits themselves.

Phil likes to benefit his rich friends. It makes him feel as though he were part of that caste as well. He's not, but he thinks so. Don't be Phil. Be better. Be charitable. Be impactful.

Lastly, a post-introduction:

No organization has paid to be a part of this book. Inclusion was solely based on research and discovery. This is not, as they term it in the newspaper business, "edu-tainment," whereby companies pay to have the newspaper write something nice about them (or they write it themselves). This is the real thing. The companies were chosen specifically because they get it, nothing more. If you're as impressed with them as I was, send them a healthy donation.

They get it.

Foreword

I distinctly remember the first time I read an Alan Harrison blog in *ArtsJournal*. My first reaction was, "Who is this guy? He actually said the quiet part out loud." My second thought was – "Oh, thank god, I am not crazy." Here is an example of a truth teller: Alan holds up a clear standard of ethics, as well as offering a step-by-step analysis of how to do better.

I have been involved in the arts for over 60 years, and nonprofits for about 50 years. I have a unique perspective, as a volunteer, donor, working with my husband to create first-in-the-nation programs aimed at inner-city kids, and finally by founding Dance Data Project®. Most of my training was in Chicago, a uniquely layered philanthropic environment where block-by-block organizations are celebrated (think President Obama and Back of the Yards), all the way up to citywide initiatives worthy of the "Make No Small Plans" ethos. But, I have seen good intentions go sideways, especially when expensive consultants with a background in for-profit right-sizing are let loose on the nonprofit world assuming the template for efficiency is transferable.

Alan's central insight, at least for me, is that it's not sufficient to assess whether an organization has stayed true to the mission (which every consultant advises) but rather, and daringly, *Is the mission as stated legitimate, given that the IRS regulations require all nonprofit organizations, including those that produce performing arts, to base their activities on improving their community?*

In other words, the self-justifying "uphold standards of excellence" or "commission and produce works that seek to encapsulate our shared humanity and ignite questions regarding the most pressing issues facing society today" just doesn't cut it. As Alan would say "Okay, so this is more blah-blah-blah to hide the fact that (insert whatever theater, dance, music company or museum) is producing art so rich people can pay for special access."

From personal observation, I can say — It ain't gonna be easy. But, yelling over and over "the arts are crucial" or "you must fund us before we go under" just doesn't play well post-Covid and is sounding very worn and decidedly privileged in a country with horrific health issues, a migration crisis, and lack of care for seniors and little ones. I can state unequivocally from personal experience that most of the donor class has little to no patience for the performing arts. I am here to report, outside of the bubble, pretty much no one cares. Really.

Of the final full year cohort of The Philanthropy Workshop (TPW), which is a global network designed to train the next generation of philanthropic leaders, I was the only member focused on the performing arts at all. My fellow cohort members were considering projects around education, creation of new vaccines, solving homelessness, creating clean water supplies, and education of girls in Africa and Asia and use of technology to create better health outcomes whether in rural America or globally. To be honest, I got fairly obvious derision. Cue the "Okay, Boomer" eye roll.

Current philanthropy in the US, particularly that originating on the West Coast, is being led by a group of entrepreneurs that have made a great deal of money, quickly, in tech using the "break things and move fast" ethos. They are interested in solving "system-wide" inequalities, preferably if there is an algorithm that can measure progress. Even the legacy foundations on the East Coast, are now being steered by 40–50-year-olds whose interests, not surprisingly, skew towards the catastrophe of climate change, unequal incarceration rates, and access to health care.

Philanthropy has become both tired and big business, with MBA-trained consultants urging arts organizations to "run like a business" — the exact opposite of what they actually should be doing. My #1 Pet Peeve — the proliferation of vaguely macho "philanthro-speak" that apes private equity and venture capital — is just a meaningless shorthand that mostly serves to prop up the self-importance of those who wish they were off on Wall Street or Silicon Valley. It's become more like bad Kabuki, totally numbing. Staff members' eyes glaze over as they nod their heads vigorously at whatever New Idea or Strategic Initiative from the Good Idea Fairy imposed on them by the latest CEO or Board, knowing it will pass through without discernible impact.

"It's for the kids ... the teachers...," etc. is a mantra I have heard for the last 3 decades to excuse appalling behavior by senior staff, misuse of interns, redirection of gifts, and refusal to acknowledge the labor of scores of women.

Let's be clear, issues of self-dealing, inflated salaries, and grandiose ambitions indulged by quiescent or overly compliant boards aren't the sole province of performing arts organizations. I have been to more than my fair share of fundraisers and experienced the garish excesses of the 90s through the Noughties. Personal experience: I attended a small private school annual fundraiser that auctioned a $22k golden retriever puppy ("Oh, look, there is a litter mate ... it goes to the underbidder!" (Now there's a realpolitik lesson to teach the Next Gen.)

Whether it's United Way International, or Oxfam, GLAAD, or #TimesUp, those in charge need strict oversight. It's easy to lose your way with proximity to access and power, especially with the urging of executive search consultants who insist that "talent costs" or advise that "You aren't hiring for character; you are hiring for vision and contacts." Both of these rationalizations, I'm sorry to say, have been my misfortune to encounter.

As a board member, or even a volunteer at a performing arts organization, whether located in a gleaming temple of culture or a church basement, you are likely familiar with the sensation of having your arm twisted on a fairly regular basis — after having been locked in a room until you cough up enough money to balance the budget which no one thought was within shouting distance of doable in the first place.

It's not fun realizing you are merely a cog in a relentless fundraising machine geared to build a new headquarters, theater, or performing arts center, which then turns out to be unsustainable, leading to the artistic and executive teams announcing a new ABBA musical to leverage what we all know is the prestige work — producing some avant-garde version of Antigone that no one actually wants to see.

To make the performing arts relevant again, wholesale change is absolutely required.

Let's start with qualifications. Any good nonprofit leader has done it all, most of it with little to no glamor or acclaim; sometimes with a resounding failure. One of my favorite stories from Alan, which pretty much tells you all you know about him, is his hilarious account of starring in #7 of the greatest theatrical flops of 1986, as written up in the *New York Daily News*. Any decent performer has been through it, the terrible reviews, the sinking sensation that "it's not going to be okay."

Over and over, I have found that the arts leaders I most admire (and Alan is surely one of them) have taken tickets, cleaned up the theater (and even the bathrooms), served drinks, loaded in and out for shows, sewn costumes, worked lighting boards, and even played back-up bass when a band member turned up sick. They do what it takes, with love and respect for everyone involved. Alan has translated that experience into a moral compass and step-by-step process to bring arts back to actually serving the communities in which they operate.

So, how to do better — well, based on Alan's books I would summarize:

First: Save us, please, from the phenomenon of the Genius (almost always, FYI, male), or the "we need to hire a rockstar" impulse of board members seeking to avoid hard work, or perhaps, the often repeated but inexplicable desire to submit to a Great Leader figure (see current politics). The toxic sludge of sleaze creeps slowly into an organization.

And the result of that?

Too often, in the performing and fine arts world, outrageous, heart-breaking trauma and yes, criminality are overlooked, covered up, or dismissed because "Oh, no, he's a friend" or "You never really know what goes on" or "You have to give artistic personalities room to move." Somehow, then, it's okay to scream at staff or demand they work 80-hour weeks, because they are supposed to be devoted to this ephemeral thing called "art" as expressed by whatever leadership decrees it to be on this particular Tuesday.

Second: Keep the main thing the main thing. If it doesn't benefit your community directly, just don't do it. If whatever play, commission, program, initiative, or advocacy doesn't lead directly to a measurable impact on the lives of the least resourced in your city, town, or village, just get rid of it, despite it being a big donor or Board Chair's pet project.

As Alan says, "art is essential." It doesn't mean you or your organization are. With firefighters, law enforcement, health professionals, and local community workers losing their lives during the pandemic, working in terrifying conditions every day without a break, ever, for months at a time, stop playing the martyr. You picked this job and this profession. If it's underpaying you, or you are being abused, try to fix the system, or get out. It's not a religious calling and you're not Mother Teresa.

Third: If you cannot measure it, ditch it. Look for better and more accurate measurements. There are incredible resources utilized by social service agencies, universities, and ethical management consultants. The performing arts are in the Stone Age in terms of program and impact assessment.

Fourth: No, things aren't going to get better, just because you have had a hit production. The model is broken. It's not a tragedy if your particular pet project or legacy theater goes out of business. See above at "acting like a business" — 80% of small businesses fail. It's not the end of the world. You don't get to claim, as one arts advocacy organization has done, that its staff "are frontline workers," thereby deserving of taxpayer supported, months-long personal assessment and refreshment.

Far too many organizations exist past their useful "sell by" date and become zombie charities mostly devoted to ensuring that the staff continue to be paid. For example, there were reports about a ballet company's artistic and executive directors' decision to fire their dancers during COVID to become "a presenting organization" which barely commissioned anything, yet kept ramping up their own compensation packages. And other reports about disgraced performing arts leaders who "retired" with massive buyout packages.

Finally: It keeps coming back to your board. All the goodwill in the world and the courage to change, from an artistic or executive director, won't make a lick of difference if your board members are really there to network with buddies and watch a cultural event from the velvet-roped comfort of the opera/theater/dance equivalent of a skybox.

Wealthy donors have been trained to give away money because they want to be loved or have their ego stroked. Far too many older big-ticket givers depend on development staff to service their surrogate family, lovers, or friends. Many program officers at the few remaining foundations giving to the arts are failing to do their due diligence. Too often I have seen a new cadre hired in to "create transformative change" devolve to handing out massive tranches of money to old friends, or "take care of their people," without any reference to the metrics and requirements of their own onerous application process.

There is plenty of work to be done, and no one particular group or contingent is to blame. It's going to take a concerted re-think by donors, arts workers, foundations, and consultants to return performing arts back to their communities and to craft new metrics or a measuring stick for success.

It is possible, however. As I noted at the beginning, my personal mantra is What Would Alan Do?

Elizabeth "Liza" Yntema
President & Founder
Dance Data Project®

Acknowledgements

Along with the people mentioned in the book, as well as the people mentioned in the last book and the book before that, I'd like to acknowledge the encouragement, inspiration, and wisdom I have gained from the following:

Danny Harrison, still brave, still brilliant, and the best son in the history of sons.
Donna Oslin, still brilliant, still brave, and my head-spinning partner in crime.

Shanley Aumiller
Kelly Backs
Lynnette Barkley
Molly Beecroft
Lisa Bielawa
Ava Bradley
Ben Blundell
Leslie Buddeke Smart
Cat Dragon
Daniel Dyer
Kim First-Aycock
Robert Barry Fleming
Tweed Fristoe
John Hart
Vicky Hartley
Paul Heppner
Katrin Hilbe
Tracy Hudak
Susan Karol
Mallory Kramer

Linda Lane
Steven Libman
Megan Marsden
Makia Oaks
Ken & Stella Osborne
Maria Catalina Prieto Vasquez
Suzie Shaub Black
Scott Silberstein
Karcheik Sims-Alvarado
Frank Smecker
Denise Smith
Tonia Steed
Jim Strait
Uzma Taj
George Tally
Christine Tibbetts
Steve Wagstaff
Nick Welch
Jonathan Wysong

And, as always, the hundreds more who have fallen out of what's left of my memory. Bless you all.

Michelle Auerbach (Editor) is a world builder and a community maker who uses all her geeky skills to transform what we've got to work with into a more just and loving place where more people get taken care of better. She holds an MFA in prose writing and a PhD in Transformational Leadership, with her dissertation on story as a technology for trauma-aware change for individuals, organizations, and communities. She coaches writers, edits amazing books like this one, and ghostwrites for change shapers around the world.

Chapter 1

What It Takes

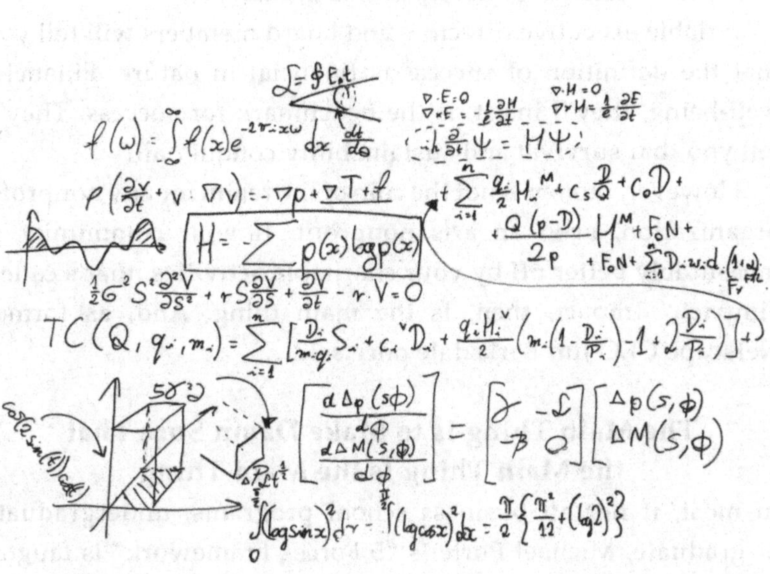

There are no easy answers to the problems facing nonprofit arts organizations in America. As it turns out, there never were. What, then, connotes success in this industry?

Pitiable executive directors and board members will tell you that the definition of success is financial in nature. Financial well-being, they'll insist, is the benchmark for success. They'll tell you that survival and sustainability conquer all.

However, money is not the coin of the realm for any nonprofit organization, even an arts nonprofit. If your community is measurably better off by your charitable activities, that's called "impact." Impact, then, is the main thing. And, as former Netscape CEO Jim Barksdale once said...

The Main Thing Is to Make Damn Sure That the Main Thing Is the Main Thing

In most, if not all business school programs, undergraduate or graduate, Michael Porter's "5 Forces Framework" is taught. It's a basic understanding of where your company is in the market. It applies to nonprofit organizations as well, with the understanding that buying and selling usually refers to underserved or unserved people in the community.

This was an exercise I actually did in a special professional development opportunity for nonprofit arts leaders at Stanford's Graduate School of Business. The "5 Forces Framework" is a sound structure, but it begat a decidedly sticky problem when we applied it to our own nonprofit arts organizations. We discovered that the Framework, a theory that should have applied to every single company we could imagine, didn't fit the model for our scope of work. Was that the fault of the time-tested framework or our own organizations?

It's a great tool for anyone opening a business. The (short and completely imperfect) descriptions of the forces are these:

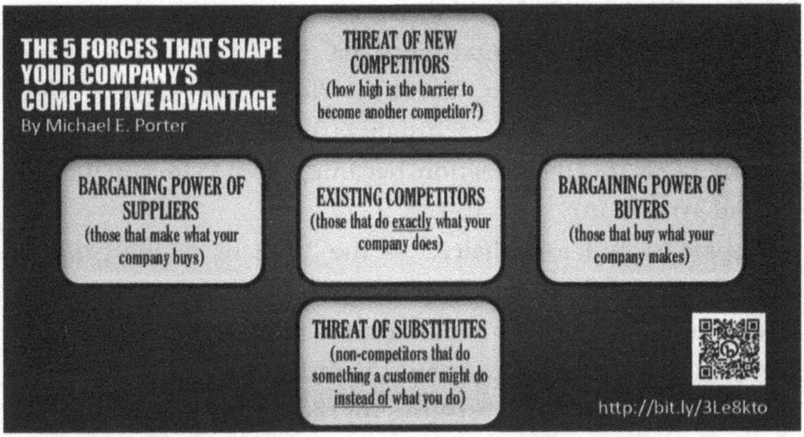

When we'd set the scope of businesses to be something like "live theaters in Kirkland, Washington," and just looked at ticket revenue as the measuring stick, it was easy.

- Existing competitors: other live theaters in Kirkland
- Bargaining power of buyers: what's the balance of power between your live theater and your ticket buyers?
- Bargaining power of suppliers: what's the balance of power between your live theater and the performers; set designers, builders, and materials; costume designers, builders, and materials, etc.?
- Threat of new competitors: is it easy or difficult for another live theater to open in Kirkland and become another competitor?
- Threat of substitutes: what other kinds of businesses might your customers choose to patronize instead of yours — every category of movies? Every category of music? Every category of dance? Every category of Opera? Every category of museum/gallery? What about just choosing to have a leisurely meal at a restaurant instead? And, of course, what about staying home and not going to see a live play?

But that didn't work. It still doesn't work.

None of the information from the first crack at the Framework took into account donor revenue, which constituted (in some arts organizations) up to 75% of the income. The thorny question became, "How do you fit that second stream in?"

As smart and experienced as the 30 of us in the program were, we could derive no good answer. Not that we didn't try, of course. Some tried to make it a six-force structure; but that really didn't work because the substitutes for donating money are different from the substitutes for seeing a play, for example. There was enough difference that shoe-horning a sixth force caused more confusion.

Others created two separate five-force structures – one for ticket revenues, the other for donated revenues. But, that took into account only the revenues and not the results from educational programs or other community issues. How do you wedge in that force? This caused some of the thinkers in the group to create multiple five-force worksheets for one company, some of which offered conflicting information on how to proceed.

What's that old saw? "A person with one watch knows what time it is; a person with two is never sure."

Now, with the passage of time, a global pandemic, and the lack of essential nature to any and every arts organization (so non-essential to the public that they're closing, causing a hue and cry ... but mostly just to arts organization people), we now know what happened.

We framed the original scope incorrectly.

A real nonprofit organization trades in impact, not revenue.

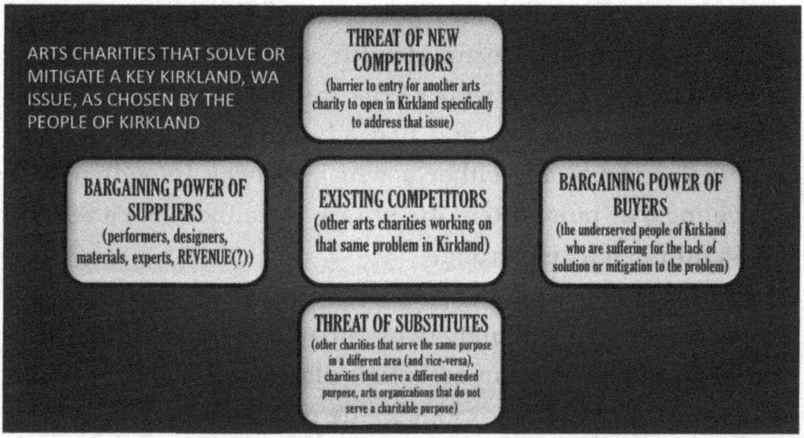

How did that change the five-force structure? Let's say that the scope is now "arts charities that solve or mitigate a key Kirkland, Washington, issue, as chosen by the people of Kirkland" and you run a nonprofit company that happens to produce live theater.

Toss that around for a while. For example, what if revenue were considered a necessary supply to achieve impact rather than the goal? Who has greater power in the relationships between your company (in the same box as "existing competitors") and each of the other forces?

There is no panacea for the ills of the nonprofit arts organization problems of today. Nor is there a need for one. Usually, the unrelenting forces of the free market, sheer mismanagement, vanity, or bad advice are enough to exorcize bad companies from the market. Usually, even among other charities, there are signs that point to impactfulness and those that point to non-impactfulness. Usually, non-impactfulness undergoes a corrective process by the charity, or else the market will eliminate it as ineffective or obsolete. After all, considering the strict definition of productivity is "the elimination of anything that is unproductive," the definition of impactfulness must be "the elimination of anything that is non-impactful."

Evidently, this news has not reached the powers that be in the nonprofit arts sector. In our sector (in which I have about 30 years of experience) exist myriad examples of sheer mismanagement, vanity, and bad advice. The notion of "best practices" has become either a whisked-away impediment to gut feelings, or more often, the phrase is donned like a Speedo at a wedding: it's just wrong.

The issues of rampant elitism, accepted toxicity, and non-acknowledgement of these organizations as public charities have determined the non-essential, dispensable, and frivolous nature of these venerable clods in the market.

If your organization is a venerable clod, tromping through the city continuously begging for money to support "the art" (even though you don't really care about "the art" – you only care about "*your* art"), then you probably still don't understand why no one is coming to the rescue. Don't they know, don't they care, you think to yourself. After all, don't they know that the production of your version of art is what's keeping the planet turning and, as such, is deserving of unending bagfuls of money, even at the expense of charities that are designed to save lives, improve working conditions, and mitigate climate change?

You quote Churchill, who reportedly said, in reply to a recommendation to cut arts funding in favor of the war effort, "Then what are we fighting for?" Of course, about 30 seconds of research shows that Churchill never said that and the entire story is bogus. Somebody made it up.

But it's a nice story (lie). "Best Practices" might say that it's good to propagate nice stories (lies) to back up your arguments. It's like telling your kids who are failing math that Einstein failed math, too.

Which, of course, he didn't. He was conversant in college physics by the age of 11.

In order to build a successful nonprofit arts sector – all performing, literary, and visual arts organizations that choose to become 501(C)(3) corporations – it is incumbent on the organizations themselves to deserve funding.

The only way in which any charity of any kind deserves funding is by producing measurable, quantifiable results.

Not just any results, mind you. These results must prove that the charity's work improves their community in any of the several tax-exempt activities listed in the IRS code under 501(C)(3). It may *receive* funding when not achieving charitable results, but it cannot *deserve* funding unless it satisfies this requirement:

> The exempt purposes set forth in section 501(c)(3) are charitable, religious, educational, scientific, literary, testing for public safety, fostering national or international amateur sports competition, and preventing cruelty to children or animals. The term charitable is used in its generally accepted legal sense and includes relief of the poor, the distressed, or the underprivileged; advancement of religion; advancement of education or science; erecting or maintaining public buildings, monuments, or works; lessening the burdens of government; lessening neighborhood tensions; eliminating prejudice and discrimination; defending human and civil rights secured by law; and combating community deterioration and juvenile delinquency.
>
> — Internal Revenue Service

And if you're kidding yourself into believing that your arts organizations serves an "educational" purpose, or even that it advances "education or science," you deserve a medal for chutzpah. Do you test for results or just hope for the best? If the former, great. If the latter? You're guessing.

In the end, calling your company "educational" when there is no data that proves that your central goal was to educate constitutes a soft, non-litigable version of fraud. It's just another nice story (lie).

There is a difference between teaching and educating. Teaching is completed when the teacher orates the curriculum. There is no regard to the students at all. It is where we get the word "professor," as in "one who professes." Lecturers teach. They declaim.

Education happens when students learn the material, and not before. The onus is on the educator to ensure that the students somehow gain the knowledge they need. This holds true from pre-school teachers to those who grant doctorates.

In the case of most of the venerable cloddish nonprofit arts organizations, when they do manage to put together an education program (usually to attract funding and no other reason) teaching stands as the core activity. The idea that any nonprofit arts organization can be described as "educational," then, leads to a conclusion that most fail at their core activity — education. They might provide study guides, curriculum helpers, and even artists to speak to the class, but they do not measure if anyone has learned anything from the process. Many nonprofit arts educational programs are sad attempts to show worth without actually showing worth. The word "fraud" comes to mind.

If an IHOP franchise called itself a nonprofit organization because its core mission was to eliminate hunger, wouldn't that be fraud as well? What's the difference between people buying a ticket from a nonprofit arts organization to gain an education or buying a short stack from IHOP to eliminate their own hunger?

The answer is that a societal need must exist for the activity to be considered charitable. Commercial activity such as the buying of pancakes or tickets does not constitute a core charitable activity. The only difference between the clods and IHOP is that IHOP never suggests for one moment that its core business is charitable.

But what is charity, if not for the betterment of a community?

For that matter, what's a community?

How do you establish the needs of that community, once you figure out what it is?

Finally, how do you assess the results of your work in solving or mitigating that need?

These are basic questions whose answers should be so easy to describe that you can rattle them off without hesitation. You should know which metrics prove your success — or, at the very least, the challenges that block success. The metrics should be tangible and measurable, not hopeful or flowery. "Just the facts, Ma'am," as they used to say on *Dragnet*.

We know what a charity is. If you run a nonprofit arts organization and believe, somehow, that it is *not* a charity, think again. It is. Given that the arts are never mentioned in the 501(C)(3) statute as an acceptable tax-exempt activity, it falls on you to make sure that it is a charitable organization, the only avenue open to you.

But you received that letter from the IRS, confirming that your organization is set up as a nonprofit. Just because you got your paperwork completed doesn't mean that you're a *good* charity, worthy of a nickel. Many nonprofit arts organizations that forget their place in the community aren't worthy of that nickel. Don't let that be yours.

Are you sure about what your community entails?

It's not altogether clear that a whole passel of nonprofit arts organizations know what "community" means to their organization. They may have a dictionary definition at the ready, or some parsed-out word salad to describe the community of people they seek, but rarely do they describe the community (or communities) that they are attempting to help. Unless, of course, it's they themselves.

They're pretty good at that last one, irrelevant though it may be.

Go ahead. Try it. Say it out loud. What is the definition of "community" to your nonprofit arts organization? It may not be the community to which you claim membership. Or it might.

Many believe that "my community" and "my audience" are equivalent terms. Or "my stakeholders." They are not equivalent. In fact, your current audience may not be a part of your community at all, but instead, a cadre of White, wealthy donors who continue to pay for those Ibsen Festivals, Bartók Marathons, and the mounting of the entirety of Shakespeare's War of the Roses plays in which all the roles are played by shadow puppets. Or that 10-hour acid jazz musical based on *The Sorrow and the Pity*. Or whatever your company's supposed artistic vision may be at the moment.

On the other hand, you may have ambitions to build your community yourself. "We build community" is something found on a great jolly shipload of arts organization websites. It's an interesting notion that assumes that there is not a community already that requires your assistance. To be fair, you can and do build a community of artists, fans, and donors. But how does that help stop injustices and provide services to those members of the area who could really benefit from attention?

It really doesn't. And that's the thing.

Many nonprofit arts organizations try to wedge their way into the statute as an "educational organization." Most arts organizations fail miserably as worthy education nonprofits. Even if you tack on some education program. Why?

An education program is better defined by, say, UCLA. It has students, testing, rubrics, experts in subject matter, grading, and a full post-graduate program to help its students gain both employment and expertise in specific subjects. Like a children's theater program, it takes in tuition, but in return, UCLA offers career trajectories instead of participation certificates. Don't get me wrong: children's theater is fun and can instill some great qualities, but to call it "education" is an insult to every certified, practicing educator.

Do you test your students throughout the program or just rehearse them for a show and sell tickets to their parents? If your organization serves adults, do you test them throughout the process and quantify their progress? If not, then yours is a failing educational nonprofit. Proof of value is everything in order to deserve that aforementioned nickel. There is just no tangible proof that anyone has been educated about anything if your organization doesn't measure it. Resisting testing is a sign of lack of confidence in your company's methods and programs, not a strength. Would you want UCLA to "guess" whether its students are actually learning something?

To do any of these charitable things, you're going to need not to find a constituency (like an audience), but a community (the underserved in your area). To make your arts organization indispensable, define "community" as that group of people who need help, where you can do the most charitable good. Otherwise, just be a for-profit corporation and be done with it and let the real charities reap some of the philanthropic money that can go directly to helping those who need it, not just those who want it.

Now that you've identified your community, it's time to identify exactly where you can help, what the goal of that help is, and the metrics for measuring success. You're going to need to establish intermittent, infinite goals. As an example, your goal may be to lift your community out of poverty caused by the homeless crisis. You can help by providing art (performed or otherwise) as a tool to provide dignity toward the unhoused population in your area, all the while teaming with social service nonprofits to join you on site and get shelter information, take applications for Section 8 housing, or provide clean clothes and a way to wash and shave. You can measure your worth with data: how many unhoused people found a way to a home? How many are now employed? How many used a service that helped them rebuild their lives, even if it did not result in full housing?

Then continue to gather data for long-term results. What percentage of unhoused people over a period of years gained employment? What were the results year-over-year? Remember:

the coin of the nonprofit realm is not money earned or donated. Money is not a metric. Impact is.

If you don't measure impact, it doesn't exist.

Purpose is often defined in the negative: what would the world miss if your organization did not exist? It's an easy answer when the impact is measurable. When the impact is descriptive *instead* of measurable (i.e., "art nurtures the soul"), there is no proof of charity, only talk.

To achieve a charitable purpose is not hard, but it requires several non-negotiable abilities. Without these, there is no reason for the organization to be anything but a commercial entity. With these explicitly spelled-out, nonprofit arts organizations thrive, even in a time where thriving is rare.

These abilities are intent, service, sympathy, listening without judgment, conscience, discipline, and teamwork. We will explore these in the following sections.

Intent

If there were a more apt description of the term, it would be *want to*.

The most important attribute of a successful nonprofit arts organization is that they *want to* serve the community as the charity they have agreed to be. Then, they must *intend* to do so. Not as a byproduct of its programming or as some ethereal unnamed public good. As a charity. Then, of course, they must *do it*.

At the center of it all, when a nonprofit organization chooses to act like a for-profit arts organization and seeks acclaim and profit over impact, then, they have shown no intent to do charitable work. When they have shown no intent to do charitable work as the main purpose of their company, they clearly have no reasonable standing as a nonprofit. And when they have no standing as a nonprofit, they should withdraw from the nonprofit sector entirely.

The rules of nonprofit work are the same for arts organizations and blood banks, but the activities differ wildly. Now, after a hundred-year pandemic, when the general public is still wary of the kind of charity to support because there are so many that have been shown to be corrupt, been hinted to be corrupt, and been cleared of being corrupt, it is unthinkable that nonprofit arts organizations will continue to choose to beg for unearned funding instead of choosing to change direction and actually earn their charitable keep.

At the heart of every nonprofit arts organization, intent drives everything else. It has to be obvious and it has to be charitable. No one is looking for subtle answers to the community's biggest challenges. Therefore, you must ask all your constituents *why your organization exists*, not what it does. If the reason it exists is anything that talks about the paucity of arts organizations in your area, that's a lie (there are 133,000 in the US; surely, there's another near you). If the reason has to do with creating community (without defining exactly what that means in nonprofit terms), that's an obfuscation. Coffee houses create community. So do restaurants, barber shops, gaming sites, casinos, ballparks, and any drunken excuse for a Vegas convention. So do unions, bowling leagues, quilting bees, and political parties — and *those groups* can even give you the names of their members and the statistics around their creation of community.

If your nonprofit's intent has anything to do with serving or supporting art, that's worthless. Art does not need to be supported or served. Not by nonprofit organizations, anyway. *People* need to be served.

Without the intent to quantifiably make the community a better place to live – using data to prove worth – there is no purpose to most ostensibly nonprofit arts organizations except to entertain. Entertainment, while not bad, is not a charitable purpose; especially when those who are entertained are the same people who donate to the company. And that leads to the second attribute of a successful nonprofit arts organization...

Service

The general idea of service is neither charitable nor uncharitable. It's a business practice more than anything else.

But for a successful nonprofit organization of any kind, the act of selfless service to those who have traditionally not been served has to be a key element of the process. For arts organizations, that means that the current system of donors donating so that donors may benefit has to cease. The system appears nowhere else in the nonprofit sector. Nowhere.

Why not?

Because the idea of using charitable revenues – revenues borne in part by taxes paid by the citizens of the state – to pay donors to subsidize their participation is an obscenity. Rather than just letting it go at that, here's how that works, in photo form, because I'm told that sometimes people are confused by words on a page:

Now do you understand what's wrong?

Let's try and decipher the meaning together. Taxpayers pay taxes. That's why they're called taxpayers. Anyone who pays taxes, including minimum wage workers who are one week's pay from eviction, is a taxpayer.

Tax-exempt companies (nonprofits who have a letter from the IRS confirming their 501(C)(3) status) are exempt from paying some taxes. That includes every nonprofit arts organization, including the Goodman Theatre in Chicago, pictured above, which spent about $23 million in the 2023–24 season — 4% of which was spent on "Education and Engagement."

Beneficiaries are those that receive subsidized services. That includes everyone who buys a ticket; because of that "tickets cover only 50% of our costs, so we have to raise money to keep the costs down" scheme.

Sometimes, nonprofit arts organizations attempt to justify tax-exempt status by pointing out that "Through the Goodman's education and engagement programs, 3,000 young people and lifelong learners participated in 10 education programs, completely tuition-free [according to the company's own annual report]."

$23 million spent. 3,000 people served. Does that seem like effective, efficient service to the underserved to you?

This lack-of-charitable-impact issue, of course, is not the provenance of the Goodman Theatre. Almost *all* nonprofit arts organizations work like that. Even those whose main beneficiaries are (usually rich, White) children. The underserved are seemingly never the prime beneficiaries of most nonprofit arts organizations.

The current model has the potential to become riddled with toxic elitism. And guess what? It *is* riddled with toxic elitism.

In most nonprofit arts organizations, donors donate so that donors may attend. Donations offer the ticket-buyer a natural subsidy to make the cost of tickets more affordable, for example (not "affordable," mind you — just "*more* affordable"). Rich people benefit from that subsidy.

In most nonprofit *non-arts* organizations, donors donate so that a certain group of people may lift their lives up from the insecurities and basic human needs that otherwise doom them to pain. Whether that group suffers from terminal illnesses and seeks a cure; or historic inequities and seeks a remedy, the people of need are centered in the process. Not the nonprofit corporation. Not its executives, staff, or board. Certainly not the donors.

Is it any wonder that arts funding is always under threat and generally diminishing? Endangered funding is not because of obscene art or controversy. It's because of the obscene practice of using taxpayer money and tax-deductible donations to serve rich folks.

As a nonprofit organization of any kind, you have to care about the plight of the people in your community. That *should* be a "goes without saying" comment, but alas, so many leaders lack the gene that offers any version of the next attribute to anyone but themselves.

Sympathy

While sympathy toward one's fellow man — let alone empathy — seems like an obvious necessity (because why would one try to do something for the sake of others if one were not altruistic in some way), too many arts organizational leaders wear blinders big enough to drive Secretariat into a brick wall when it comes to thinking about the less fortunate, at least on an organizational level.

Yes, arts organizations (both commercial and nonprofit) picked up the call when AIDS was killing artists *because* AIDS was killing artists. Ebola received no such movement, even though it was even more deadly. As for AIDS, producers, purveyors, and performers have been powerfully steadfast in their support. Did they act in similar manners when COVID was killing people — far more than ever died in the AIDS crisis years of the 1980s? The answer is not an obvious yes.

The financial plea during the AIDS crisis was to raise money to find a cure, treat the sick, and save the dying. The plea during the COVID crisis years of 2020–2022 was a "return" to performance. Most arts organizations used the time to find ways to gain revenues, to use national emergency funding efforts to keep their companies going (and keeping themselves paid), and to shriek against any precautions that endangered audience members, artists, and the like. Even with strict testing demanded by the unions, there were dozens of organizations — even those led by smart, caring leaders — who believed that the path back was too slow to develop, despite all the deaths and infections. To those few COVID deniers, the appropriate actions to combat a deadly virus were the key reasons for the financial hellhole in which they now find themselves.

Ignoring, of course, the dozen years of reduced funding before the pandemic. Whose fault was that?

It's easier to blame bad acts on the pandemic itself, and even then, to disregard its devastation to … to … to what, exactly? To bring back performances? Seems like a trifling, selfish reason with little sympathy toward the general public or its collective needs. Let alone those that suffer from health inequity, such as the entire Black population of the United States.

Instead, the industry provided self-serving cuteness.

"This is Just Intermission - Paramount Theatre, Seattle" by SounderBruce is licensed under CC BY-SA 4.0.

The message presented here on this marquee was too clever by half. Instead of showing sympathy to people who were frightened to collect in groups (in this case, in the city of Seattle), or showing deference and thanks to "essential workers" (a term the general public and press used to describe people whose jobs kept people connected and served *even when it put their own lives at risk*), all it did was relate to the public that the nonprofit arts organization that housed these plays and musicals would be back in business soon. That's the opposite of sympathetic — selfish, self-centered, and based in a belief that its artistic product served the community. People were dying all over Seattle, but heck, the Paramount would be back after intermission?!

Consider the March 25, 1911, fire in the Triangle Shirtwaist Factory in Greenwich Village, New York. Would it have been sympathetic for the owners of the building to put out a sign that said, "DON'T WORRY! WE'LL BE BACK MAKING SHIRTS SOON!"? Or would that have been a total insult to the 146 workers who lost their lives, their families, and the network of people who worked in nearby unsafe conditions? Or is that just the consequence of runaway capitalism?

So, if you are not already sympathetic to the plight of those in need in your community, get there. If you don't *want to,* see the first ability in this section. As a nonprofit arts organization with an industry-wide horrible reputation as money-grubbing non-charitable charities, you have no time to waste on your own First World problems.

To justify your organization's status as a public asset, (let alone as the charitable asset it promised to be when it applied for its 501(C)(3) designation from the state), the first thing to do is ask all the leaders in your own community to break down its problems and issues. Then, using art as a tool to do so (as the companies in this book have done), do nothing but that. Art is a terrific tool when used as such and not as an instrument of vanity or appeasement. Why waste a moment doing vanity work (that opera that will sell out the house; that all-female version of *Coriolanus* that proves it's anything but a dud; that all-Black version of *Pacific Overtures*; etc.) when people are in trouble? If art, all by itself, is a powerful tool to encourage self-expression, build confidence, and deregulate stress, why aren't you giving it to those who need it most – for example, that single mom raising three kids, all of whom live in a 2003 Corolla?

Why would you care what any critic were to say about the *je ne sais quoi* of your artistic prowess when people in your town need help? And, if your work becomes indispensable to the community – which should be your goal – why even invite a critic to come? Wouldn't it be better to publicize the results of your charitable work instead of the somewhat irrelevant artistic process?

To gain sympathy, there is one attribute you need desperately. It's much harder than it sounds. You require the ability to listen without judgment.

Listening (without Judgment)

Listening is not "hearing." It is not sitting forward in your chair and staring at the bridge of the nose of the person talking (that's called "*acting* like you're listening"). It has nothing to do with the nod of your head or the language of your body. Listening is the first part of gaining understanding – understanding of your community's needs, your purpose as a charity, and your place in the people's ecosystem.

Those in the Deaf community – those who identify as part of the signing community, regardless of their hearing levels – are, perhaps ironically, among the best listeners among us. Dame Evelyn Glennie, in a 2003 Ted Talk in Monterey, California, is a deaf percussionist. Her job, however, as she states it is this: "My job is all about listening. And my aim, really, is to teach the world to listen."

Watch an American Sign Language (ASL) interpreter closely, especially when they have room to work. The words spoken elsewhere — words that mean a lot to someone, or else the company probably would not have even considered to have an interpreter on hand — turn into a vibrant, emotional dance from the interpreter. While a speaker tends to hide his or her emotions, the interpreter has the power to amplify them — and yes, the word "amplify" is used on purpose. Forced to listen to the meaning (and not just the words), ASL interpreters add a layer of understanding that a simple conversation may not.

When you are sitting with a community leader and seeking input on what issues are the kinds that your arts organization can tackle, what kind of results you want to achieve, and why your company is exactly the right company to tackle these issues, think of yourself not as someone across the table, but as an interpreter.

Challenge the community member (so as not to fall into any trap of a "pet project" or a "personal gripe") by asking deeper and deeper questions about the results. Reframe questions as you hear them, just to make sure that their words match their meanings. And if they don't, do it again, with gusto. Be excited about helping instead of being "professional" (listless and undemonstrative so as not to lose face). Professionalism, the way it is now interpreted, has nothing to do with demeanor or problem-solving. It has to do with keeping temperatures low, playing it cool, formality, and stoicism.

Having said that, can you name a dominant American racial/ethnic/religious group that prizes stoicism and calls it "professionalism"?

Yup. The White folks. The Puritans. The privileged. To these folks, let me remind you that using the tools of the White folks does not make the problems go away. They tend to exacerbate the problems. They ask others to adapt to impassiveness, and thoughtlessness disguised as thoughtfulness. They treasure the idea of "rising above the fray," instead of diving straight down into it.

These are the kinds of problems that lead many White nonprofit arts leaders to believe that they are not equipped to deal with the problems of their communities, even though they could be. It leads them to the conclusion that while their organization might be a charity on paper, that's really just a business classification and nothing more (untrue). They see their problems as dire because previous strategies that relied on privileged behavior are no longer effective and they have no other arrows in the quiver.

Look at your own nonprofit arts organization. What pressing charitable issues in your community are you addressing? If you don't know, ask someone. And listen – really listen – to the response. It may include some resentment for never having thought of addressing them before. That's on you, not them.

To react positively to your listening sessions, you'll likely have to put aside your previous notions of allyship and helpfulness. Your organization is not neutral in the plight of those that need help, nor is it incapable of offering services. But you may feel put out by the idea that nonprofit work is actually harder than mounting the latest Off-Broadway hit or the hottest Mahler symphony. That extra weight on your company's back might lead your leaders to believe that it is not their job to do charitable work.

That's an understandable feeling, which is why the last attribute required to run a successful nonprofit arts organization has to do with what happens inside your collective hivemind when no one is looking.

Conscience

Having a conscience often means that you do know the difference between charity and commercial ends. In the arts, it likely means that you care more about the people you serve in your community who need the help than you do your board, donors, staff, artists, and yourself. To you, "service above self" is not a Rotary Club motto, but a way of life.

The act of doing charitable programs at a charity shouldn't sound so difficult to implement, but at a nonprofit arts organization, the waters are often too choppy. It takes a lot of energy to navigate them, and too often, it is the leaders with a strong conscience who take the fall when things don't go perfectly well in the first five minutes. Having a conscience, all by itself, is likely not enough to succeed. You need to have an internal guide that speaks to the results. The impact your company promised as a charitable organization — even if it never used the phrase in all the documents set forth by your state — must take place, and clearing the conscience of years of neglect is a key step to making that happen.

So, with conscience, you also need a goldfish memory and the strength that comes from knowing that what you're doing is better for everyone. Conscience and guts, the combination that will keep your company on the right track.

It's difficult to maneuver your craft when the lake has more alligators than water. The best thing to do is to continue to do the right work. After all, you're doing exactly what a charitable organization is supposed to do.

Serve the people. Especially those who have been so greatly un-served. Your conscience, if it's in good working order, will compel you to choose greatness over survival, no matter how much others will bridle against that notion. The fate of your nonprofit arts organization, even if the art is "excellent" or has "meaning," does not lie in its mere continuance. It lies in your company's determination to, when faced with options, choose the ones that lead to a better public.

Allowing the toxic donor class — those elitists who believe that there is no problem at all with donors being the beneficiaries of their own donations — to define "sustainability," which they mis-define as "survival," is of prime concern. Let's be clear: sustainability is not survival, no matter how many times a dying organization may say that it is.

The Toxics rally around the notion of keeping on keeping on, no matter how little the impact on the community, because they believe they are at the heart of the solution, not the problem. This is the way of privilege. When a ruling class is challenged as to its motivations, or is asked to lift people up out of unsafety and insecurity (below the lowest level of Maslow's Hierarchy of Needs), they require the continual pat on the back for their bestowing of gifts. They need a plaque, a special room, and constant thank-yous.

Not every donor — or even large-scale donor — acts in this manner. Some give, expect the thank you (not unreasonable), and just want to know how things are going. They don't want to be continually asked for money, nor do they want a relationship based on financial dependence. Like many people, they want a relationship based on evidence of worth, just as you do. They don't want two-hour lunches, they don't want to be coddled, and they don't generally want name recognition everywhere (even if their name recognition encourages others to give). They want information. They want impact. If they have access to your company's leadership, it is not to talk about the next artistic event — it is to talk about what they can do to help bring impact to the society.

It is only when your company chooses not to have charitable impact at its center that the only donors you will attract are those who only want their shoes shined. To keep that mindset in the forefront of your company, you'll need a difficult attribute, one that is not malleable.

Discipline

The most successful nonprofit arts organizations in the country are those that have the discipline to navigate their work by the north star of charitable impact. The programs may change as times themselves change; the delivery systems of the art may change with the communities, but the choice to provide impact never changes. It is never set aside, not even for short-term financial gain. In fact, when opportunities arise to expand, it is the communities' need for expanded activities that guide the operations, not the search for money.

Doubling down on impact shows discipline. Doubling down on "artistic excellence" shows organizational insecurity and rudderlessness. Doubling down on using the financial bottom line as a metric for success shows a lack of knowledge as to what a charity is supposed to do.

When I brought the "Under 25? Only $10!" program to Seattle Repertory Theatre in 1997 (my group at Pittsburgh

Public Theater had invented the idea three years earlier), we expanded our youth audience from 1,200 season-long "student rush" tickets to 12,000 "under 25" tickets. By year three, the audience of those under the age of 25 had increased to almost 20,000. The elegance of the program – tickets for anyone under the age of 25 were $10 each, no restrictions whatsoever, including when the tickets were purchased, how they were purchased, and where the seats were located – caused the audience to be filled with those who never thought they could afford a ticket. That program alone caused an increase in the attendance numbers of those with high aspirational education and lack of funds (pre-law students, MA candidates in English, first-year educators, etc.). It was, at its core, an anti-elitist program created to draw long-term interest, not merely a discount program.

Educational aspiration is the most valuable predictor of audience participation, not wealth. It just so happens that educational aspiration is also the most valuable predictor of wealth (down the line), so it is easy for unskilled nonprofit arts leaders to mistake the two. Ask yourself: is it harder to get a high-school educated cattle millionaire to attend an opera than a semi-broke graduate student in the English department? The answer, usually, is yes. Money, therefore, is not the determining factor. Educational aspiration is.

That said, it was a program that had long-term goals that were also based in giving back. Unfortunately for all, after I left the company, the program fell into the hands of those that did not understand its purpose – the development department.

The original plan called for this: after a critical mass of participants were to reach 25 years of age, the offer would be "extended" for that year as a favor to the patron. It would be at that point that they would receive word (at the time from emails and letters – now it would be through varying social media) that they were eligible to receive an easy, small commitment, inexpensive set of season tickets through age 30 (for example, 3 plays for $49, up to 2 sets per person). The idea here followed the research that by age 25, these same high-education students would be at the beginning of their wealth track, might be into long-term relationships, and might become attracted to some of the other perks of season ticket packages (discounts on restaurants nearby, discounts on additional tickets, the ability to exchange tickets at no charge, etc.).

Then, at the age of 30, by virtue of having attended for more than five years, a few realities will have come to pass. The patron, now an independent wage earner, might well be able to afford a season ticket package, and want to do so, given the regular attendance over such a long, impressionable period. If the patron were not making enough money, by then they would have become familiar with single-ticket discounts (Entertainment publications, for example). And finally, given their status, this would have been the time to begin the conversation to subsidize the next generation of "Under 25s" with a financial gift.

What actually happened was that the program was curbed and a new program to increase the number of *wealthy* young "professionals" began. Composed mostly of the children of board members and high donors, this collective became an outrageous country club of toxicity. The members of the club, seeking exclusivity and perks, perks, perks, just continued the legacy of country club attendees for which Seattle Rep had become so well known.

The original program was deemed unsuccessful (despite the revenues and numbers) because the money-grubbers were unhappy when not enough rich, White folks were having their *glutei maximi* osculated to their expectations.

Here's where discipline might have helped. If I, as the leader of the marketing and communications contingent, had gained more one-on-one buy-in by showing the results not in numbers or revenue (which was always the first question) but by the impact for the future of these participants, it would have been more difficult to dismantle. If we had been stronger advocates for the power of art to change the future for insecure young people, the program would have been even more successful, all the way to the donation portion.

That was on us, both as a department, and on me as its leader. I left, opening the door for toxicity to flood in where it had been notably absent. The department was trampled by those in higher positions (older board members, the development director, etc.) who believed that dollar signs represented the company's most important metric. Today's dollars are never an important metric of success, even when they're high. The long-term value of a younger generation choosing to spend time going to an art form might be considered a metric, but not financially.

Let me be clear on this: revenue is never a metric of success for a nonprofit organization, arts or otherwise. Never. It's not a publicly traded corporation on the New York Stock Exchange. It's a different kind of corporation altogether, one in which the measure of success is determined by the impact on the community it serves. If there is a measurable impact (better education, fewer issues stemming from a housing crisis, eradication of food insecurity, etc.), something that can use actual data (not just anecdotes or national survey answers) to prove that the world is better for having had your nonprofit organization in your community, then yours is achieving success. If not, then not.

Sadly, the managing director of Seattle Rep at the time was a brilliant individual with a single blind spot; pride for the fact that the company had never had a single annual deficit during the time they presided in that position.

So, when we discuss discipline as a core characteristic, we don't mean the style of the art. We don't mean the choice of artistic material (by itself). We don't even mean the financial discipline not to run a deficit, or to recover from a long-term deficit. Taking the previous image to heart, none of that matters. But if you maintain your discipline toward making the lives of your community better — either by providing them services they cannot receive anywhere else (that you can measure) or by compelling participants to increase equitable activities, especially for those who were born into inequity (by virtue of skin color, socioeconomic circumstances, or ethnic hate) — and you use art as a singularly effective tool to do so, your organization becomes worthy of that nonprofit status. Until then, your nonprofit arts organization is just spinning its wheels, taking up space, and hoovering contributions from charities that walk the walk.

Teamwork

Intent, service, sympathy, listening, conscience, and discipline. You will find no classes on these subjects at your expensive MFA program in arts administration. Nor should you – these are innate qualities that must be present for your company to succeed.

There are more than 1,000 reasons for a nonprofit arts organization – nascent or experienced – to fail. There is only one reason for it to succeed. Ironically, that reason has little to do with the art, as we've uncovered in this chapter.

The truth is that few people have the requisite amounts of intent, service, sympathy, listening, conscience, and discipline to make an organization successful. Some have some. Others have others. But if, as a group, you can lean on each other to emphasize those six characteristics so that, as a single nonprofit arts organization working together, all of those things come to pass, you have the best chance to succeed.

That requires teamwork, which is not as simple as reading one chapter of a Jim Collins book and deciding to put the right people on the bus. For a nonprofit arts organization to succeed, you require people who innately have at least half of the key attributes. If a decision-making leader has only one or two, you'll have dangerous power struggles. While that's a natural happenstance of most teams, it becomes a problem when the path to success is so narrow for anyone tackling this industry.

Under the "it should go without saying" portion of this chapter, you need people who have all the requisite skill sets to do their tasks successfully, whether that has to do with board tasks, artistic tasks, administrative tasks, reporting tasks, development tasks, marketing tasks, etc. In a small company, a few people do multiple tasks. That can be appealing to some — those who see that as a way to keep the mission on point — but can overwhelm others, especially those with families.

On that last point, let's be frank (as though we haven't been already?). The leadership of nonprofit arts organizations cannot be so time-consuming as to exclude people with families. That goes not only for women (although it is held against them more keenly for merely having the *potential* of bearing children), but for men as well. If a leader is working a 168-hour week, there are multiple problems afoot. When you have a team of people working toward a charitable goal, those problems can be mitigated somewhat.

But you cannot go into the business of running a nonprofit arts organization (or any company, really) by celebrating burnout. If you cannot take a vacation, you are working too many hours. If you are paid, ostensibly or otherwise, for a 40-hour week, work 40 hours. Even leaders cannot be everywhere, nor do you want them to be.

On the other side of that argument: just because someone sends you an email when you're not on the clock doesn't mean you have to read it. If you're the company's leader and you haven't empowered those on call to handle minor emergencies without your input, you are a lousy team player. Get yourself some therapy to discover why you have trust issues.

Whether you're the executive director or a volunteer usher, you have office hours to complete your tasks. If you cannot complete them in the time allotted, fix that. Adding to your stress will only exacerbate the problem and shorten your career (and lifespan). The reward, especially when it is non-charitable in nature, is not even close to being worth the risk.

Lastly, on a tangent: if you are spending your off-hours in straight recuperative mode for your on-hours, *you are still at work*. I know many people who come home exhausted from their jobs. Often, they are not in control of their own schedules and have agreed to take on everything in order to look like a "good worker." That is rewarded by, well, not much.

And when they come home, they plop down on the couch, eat some fast food, and sleep until morning.

That's not a life. That's life in service to your job (not a job in service to your life). If we learned nothing else from the pandemic, we learned that time is precious. Don't spend all your waking *and sleeping* hours in service to your job. It hurts you, which hurts the company, which hurts the needy, which hurts the community, which hurts everybody.

You may think working until you drop is some star on your personal epaulet. Or that it will go in your "permanent record." It's not. It won't. But it might cost some time off your life.

Engaging people for a team (instead of just an organizational chart) requires the provision of professional educational skills at regular periods. In the nonprofit business, this is especially true because circumstances surrounding the people in your community change with the wind. (Sometimes, that's a literal sentiment, given the increase of hurricanes from over-high ocean temperatures caused by global climate disaster.)

But even when analyzing your own company's resource allocation by using the generally accepted business tools of the day, you can run into trouble when you don't really know what it is you do. That's where your team comes in — to set everyone straight that your company is, in fact, a charity. Concentrate on this: your company has the status and ability to make the world a better place for entire communities of people who need your help. Do that.

Do that, and you'll achieve the sort of success that the organizations in this book have received. Like theirs, it may not be permanent nor might it outlive the unique leaders that head each one. You might need some additional changes to make it work even better. But still, these are organizations to be envied, to be studied, and whose most important attribute is that they care about the plight of the people in their home communities. Everything else, to them, is secondary. That's what makes these nonprofits a better buy in today's donation market. It's what makes them a player in the civic leadership market. It makes them indispensable — the most important, long-lasting, and (incidentally) fundable attribute of all.

Chapter 2

Behold LO: The Louisville Orchestra

My vision for Kentucky is a Commonwealth where there is so much economic opportunity, and our quality of life is so high, that people who are born here can stay here, and people who aren't fortunate enough to be born in Kentucky, can look forward to locating here.

— Ernie Fletcher

Teddy Abrams, center, Music Director of the Louisville Orchestra

Louisville, Kentucky. Bourbon, bats, and basketball. Mint juleps, fast horses, and outlandish hats. Among the walls at Muhammad Ali International Airport, this mural caught my eye:

The caption reads, "This is an arts town, so touches of brilliance are everywhere, from our stages and museums to our festivals and skyline. Music in a park. Painting on a street corner. Dancing wherever it feels right. Louisville lives and loves the arts."

Remembering that this is an ad for, essentially, loving the city of Louisville, it struck me that the populist art described in words had little to do with the institutional art shown in three out of the four images. The one on the right, for example, is of Teddy Abrams, the music director of the Louisville Orchestra (LO). He's made the remarkable decision to bring music to the people of Kentucky, not the other way around.

Almost 800,000 people live in Louisville, of whom about 550,000 are adults. Before you consider your preconceived notions about people living south of the Mason-Dixon line, just know that 20% of them have attained a bachelor's degree and 13.5% more got their master's, Doctorate, or other advanced Graduate degree. That's just about equal to the statistics found in the US Census database for 2020 for the whole country.

I'm sure some of you are surprised that folks in Appalachia, in which the first and third "a" is short, as in a Louisville Slugger "bat," (not the "bait" you put on the end of your hook at Hardin Lake), are just as educated as everyone else in the country. More educated than half, less educated than half. Then again, I'm sure some of you don't quite understand what's been going on in Louisville or the rest of Kentucky.

Louisville faces very similar issues to most other cities in this country. It's profoundly segregated. Historically, and even now, there's still quite a bit of mistrust of the police. It has not healed from, nor has it forgotten the tragedy of the police murder of Breonna Taylor, and who knows if it ever will? For Black people to trust a system that has worked against them — and still does in the twenty-first century — there has to be a moment to process responsibility, justice, and equity. It continues to take too much time to achieve, and for status quo lovers in Kentucky, that's what they bank on.

There's a lot of mistrust between the people and metropolitan governments. That goes for liberals and conservatives alike. There's a lot of yelling and trolling and not a hell of a lot of listening in the state of Kentucky. The arts have the ability to change that narrative, which is why they struggle, both financially and through the evil grapevine of gossip and innuendo. A lot of challenges have plagued all of the arts organizations in town, individually and collectively. The artists, too, have struggled, individually and collectively.

There are several arts organizations in Louisville. They fall into the typical American city setup: one large theater company, one large orchestra, one large ballet, one opera, etc. All struggling for solvency, slow to change, and considering anti-competitive emergency funding apparatuses. Except one, as we'll detail in this part of the book.

There are several more members of the arts community, of course. Eighty-one arts organizations, including venues and purveyors, took part in an Americans for the Arts survey that depended on their labor in collecting data from arts patrons.

Oh, would that the survey had also included non-arts patrons, of which there are a higher number, but that's Americans for the Arts' research problem, not mine.

If you don't think there's a difference, consider the following activity. You've just enjoyed an expensive dinner at a highly regarded restaurant in your neighborhood. After a few days, someone contacts you *from that restaurant* to ask you if you agree with the statement, "This restaurant is an important pillar for me within my community." Given that "important" can mean anything from "crucial" to "notable," the question stands unanswerable. Yet, when a response is requested from the people that served you dinner, one that you enjoyed, you're likely to say, "yes."

That explains why 81.1% of arts patrons in the City of Louisville or Jefferson County responded that they tended to agree with the statement, "This venue or facility is an important pillar for me within my community." Oddly, the question asked about the "venue or facility," not the organization performing in it or the art that was performed. Back to the restaurant analogy, the question was not about the food or the skill of the chef, but the restaurant in which it was served.

As often happens with research projects about the arts, the work was expensive, but not extensive. And confusing as hell.

There is definitely an approach to the arts in Louisville that uniquely speaks to the character of the people who live and have lived there. Louisville, after all, was a Union city in what has become a Confederate state. It is both segregated and integrated, both safe and dangerous, and both quirky and utilitarian.

One arts leader told me that Louisville likes to think that it was the Switzerland of the Civil War. Considering that we now know how non-neutral Switzerland was during wartime, that might be truer than we think. If asked to pin it down, it's a city more of the

South than any other cardinal direction, although there are those who would happily change that in a second (if they could).

As such, Louisville, where bourbon was created by charring the barrels, is both stately and wacky. It's a city, not a series of cities with myriad downtowns, like Los Angeles, Dallas, or Houston. While the large city of Cincinnati, Ohio, is only 100 miles away, Cincinnati has its own attractions and repulsions, which become evident when you discover that that city has been referred to as "where Germany meets the South."

Louisville is not Cincinnati. Louisville is Louisville. Horses race in the Kentucky Derby at Churchill Downs on the first Saturday of every May. The colleges' sports teams (the ones who wear red, not the ones who wear blue) tend to be pretty good. The Greatest of All Time was born here. Great writers are from Louisville — Pulitzer Prize-winning playwright Marsha Norman, internet storyteller Jon Bois, alphabetically obsessed detective writer Sue Grafton, and the Gonzo icon Hunter S. Thompson.

And then there's this orchestra. Welcome to the **Louisville Orchestra**.

The Louisville Orchestra is offering a cultural experience that, without the ability to come as a school, they just wouldn't have. This is a unique way for students — well, for all people, really — to connect with each other, just being able to enjoy the same things but in their own personal way. It gives them an avenue for their creativity, but mental health-wise, music is a big part to help people take a step away and just zero in on the sound.

— Elementary School Counselor

The LO won a Grammy® Award in 2024 — Best Classical Instrumental Solo (*The American Project* — Yuja Wang; Teddy Abrams, conductor). While an award is a special kind of acclaim, Abrams would give it back if it meant that they couldn't bring their music to the people — *all* the people, not just those with

Krugerrands in their Hermès Birkin bags. They are expert chefs who have prepared exquisite food — and don't insist that all of it has to be served within the same four walls of a chichi bistro. In fact, the LO would prefer to give away their version of artistic sustenance if it benefitted those who might never get it any other way.

There's a Reason England Threw Them Out

There is no singular "American" culture or music, which is why American music both leads and reflects American culture. The regions of the country define their own culture, much like the nations of Europe. When there is ebb and flow among the kinds of music played by the musicians of a particular part of society, the music can become richer, more meaningful, and demonstrably radical.

This is where music departs from culture in America, which is still dominated by all the people kicked out of Europe: the Puritans, among the only sectors of the population who came to America because the English thought they were religious wackos. Black people were stolen and enslaved. Jews ran away from being killed by Cossacks, Bolsheviks, and later, Nazis. Most other non-Puritan Whites came here because of the promise of a better life.

In Louisville, as in other parts of the US with roots in Appalachia, White native music is similar to Irish and Scottish folk music. This is not a surprise, as there were enormous numbers of Scots and Irish who migrated to this place. But the relative poverty and betrayal thrust upon the bulk of the immigrants (and their successors) by mine owners and other grifters, carpetbaggers, and politicians continues to this day. Even though coal, for example, will be phased out of use by the end of the 2030s, there is no current plan to move these extraordinarily hard-working, early dying, respiratory disease-ridden people to the industries of the energy sources that will replace coal and oil.

On the other hand, the people are generally upbeat. While all generalizations are false (joke intended), there's a strong undercurrent of "survival despite," a personal independence that leads to the notion that regardless of what happens with life, health, and politics, let's keep our family and friends close. It stems from, as one staff member of the LO put it, a Libertarian point of view, grounded in the idea that happiness comes from controlling your own life.

Not that that's always worked, but then again, nothing has *always* worked. Mitch McConnell's seemingly endless reign as the Republican party leader ended during my research time with the LO. No one was surprised (he was physically faltering) and no one was angry about it. Because, and this is a secret that most Louisvillians don't seem to want to tell you, they really couldn't stand the guy. In their minds, he too-easily changed his views to whatever was popular at any given moment.

Oh, and they think Rand Paul is as much a nutcase as you do. Still, it's the devil you know...

Just Down the Street from David and the Bat

The administrative offices of the Louisville Orchestra are on Main Street. One block away is a giant reproduction of Michelangelo's David, made of 30-foot-tall foam painted in startlingly bright gold leaf. If this book were in color, the following photo would be even more striking, but even in black and white, it's odd.

You might ask why there's a gold-painted foam statue of David on Main Street in Louisville. You wouldn't be out of your mind to ask. Like many American art oddities, it's an advertisement, this one for a hotel chain. Turkish artist Serkan Özkaya is responsible for this (re)creation. Originally a project for the Istanbul Biennial art exhibition, David unfortunately collapsed under his own weight. Özkaya salvaged and restored the statue and created two more casts, one of which was acquired by 21c Museum Hotels.

So no, there is no connection between Louisville and Florence, for example. This rendition of David is about twice the size as the original. The view from beneath it is downright frightening.

Yeesh. But this statue is dwarfed by the bat.

Scene Change 3

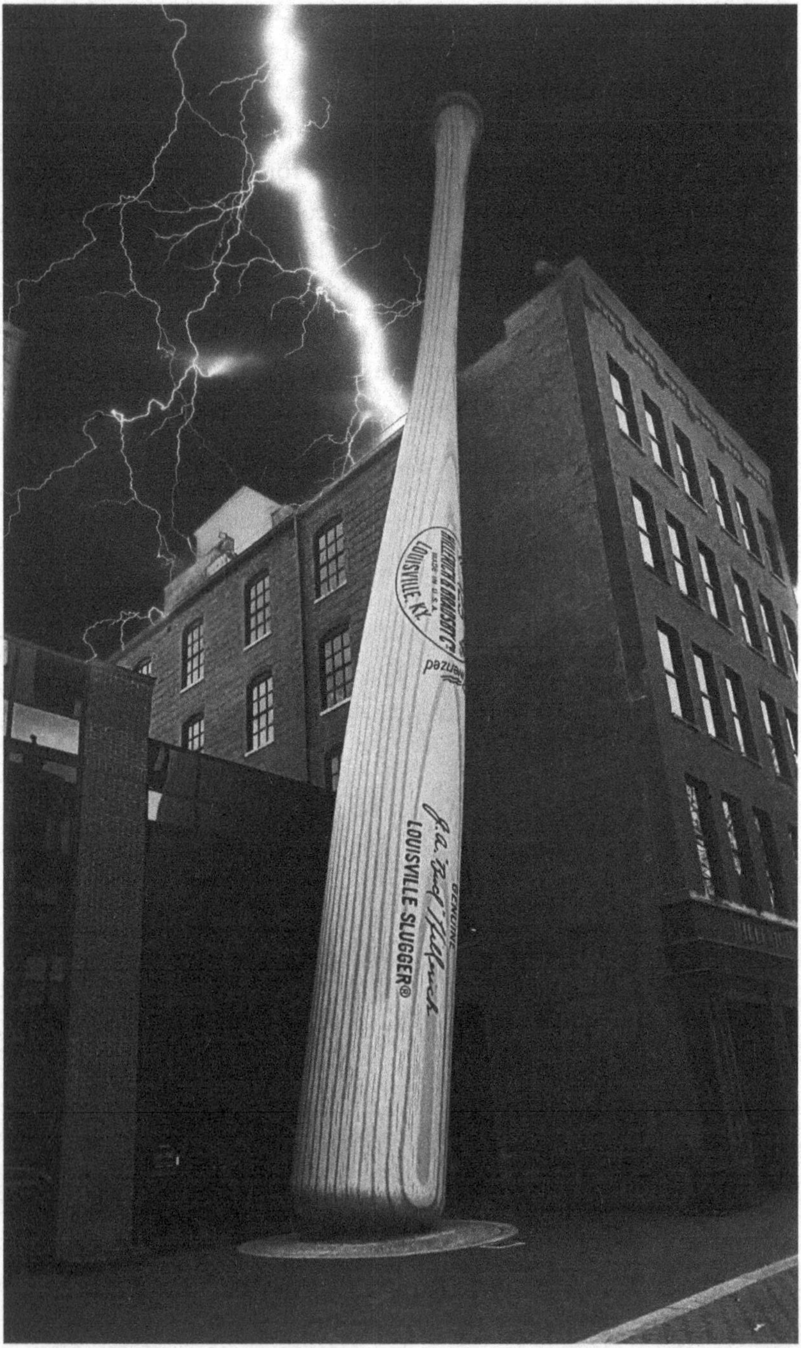

The Louisville Slugger Museum is distinguished from surrounding buildings by the 120-foot-tall baseball bat leaning against it. Erected in July 1996, the bat weighs 34 tons and is made of hollow carbon steel. Normally something this size would be a problem for the state department of transportation or break some law about signage, but the bat is also a plumbing vent for the museum's basement bathrooms.

Weird.

So when the Louisville Orchestra broke the ranks of the other large nonprofit arts organizations in the city, the weirdness of the decision did not break ranks with the soul of the city. In fact, the board's decision to hire a then-24-year-old conductor with great bona fides and put the company in his hands – and his decision to put the welfare of the people ahead of the creation of the art – was not an unusual Louisville approach to a longstanding problem.

When Your Back's Against the Wall, Break Out Your Daubers

Tonya McSorley and Nate Koch have been working with the Louisville Orchestra for a combined 44 years. McSorley is the CFO and Koch is the Chief of Staff. More than anyone else in the company – perhaps no one in the state of Kentucky – they are proudest to be working with a company that faced its demons, vamped until ready, and came out on top. McSorley, who began working at LO in the late 1990s, had seen a pattern of budgeting that, while common in the nonprofit arts sector, may easily have doomed most companies to bankruptcy.

"We have always budgeted backwards," explained McSorley, "meaning that we committed to expenses before we had the revenue in place. There was an expense budget first, after which we had to figure out how we were going to pay for it instead of the other way around. The challenge is that we work with musicians on contract in a multi-year collective bargaining agreement [CBA] that commits us to expenses three and four years out, before we've planned those seasons. The company makes a commitment to the musicians way ahead of time, even before we put the revenues on paper."

Musicians are the largest expense line on the budget. Their work is paramount to an orchestra and they deserve every penny for which they bargain. That is not the issue. No one begrudges great musicians earning a living as great musicians at the Louisville Orchestra. The issue that has popped up over the years is the distress caused by the lack of capable revenue projections in a multi-year process.

Revenue projections depend on recent history, politics, the local economy, and other factors in order to be even remotely accurate. It dooms many nonprofit arts organizations into wishful thinking on their annual budget, leading to deficits, leading to bankruptcy. That's exactly what happened.

In December 2010, the Louisville Orchestra filed for Chapter 11 bankruptcy.

"We were too big," summarized McSorley. "We were bigger than what we could afford. We had too many service weeks. We had too many players. It was too much of a high fixed cost for this organization. It had come to a head even years before that. We almost filed in 2003 and 2006."

Like many arts nonprofits in Louisville, they always struggled with cash, which is not the same thing as struggling with a budget. Cash flow is what keeps the company going, regardless of the budget. Without sufficient cash flow, they couldn't pay their bills or afford their own payroll.

"We basically were in court soon after the filing to get permission to pay bills," continued McSorley. "When you're under Chapter 11, you have to work with a financial trustee appointed by the court. That person gives you permission to pay for things."

Interestingly, in a corporate environment (which is where many of the board members at the time came from), no company would ever allow expenses to guide revenues, as the LO (and many other nonprofits) did. They would insist that revenues come first, then expenses. But that's not really the way nonprofit arts organizations work — unless they have other ways of improving the bottom financial line, especially in times of stress. McSorley and Koch told me about a fundraising effort that I don't believe I've ever experienced with a nonprofit arts organization, even though it was relatively brilliant.

In 2005, during the middle of several financial perils, the LO's board president, Joe Pusateri, went to McSorley with news from another charity in the community who had run a very successful bingo. Pusateri told her, "I want the orchestra to do this, and I need you to make it happen."

McSorley visited local bingo halls to understand the bingo world. In 2005, they had their first bingo session at a place called Bingo City — sessions that continued weekly on Thursday nights for seventeen years.

"Back then you could smoke in the bingo halls," she said, shaking her head. "Everything was yellow, the walls, the ceilings — everything. It's a cash business. I had to put controls in place to ensure that the cash balanced and that we adhered to the Kentucky charitable giving regulations."

Koch was heavily involved in the games as soon as he started at the LO in 2006:

"We would work our full-time jobs and then we would go to bingo. We were doing one bingo session a week and then it grew to two sessions on the same day, because in the state of Kentucky you can only do two gaming sessions within a week. So, we chose to do a 7:30 p.m. and midnight session on Thursdays. One year, I remember that we netted $225,000. That's money that we couldn't go out and raise elsewhere. It was just another fundraising effort that we did. And so, we carried this on until July of 2022. When we found out that we secured $4.3 million in state money for the In Harmony tour, we decided to end charitable gaming and redirect our attention to our mission, which is to go out to communities and spread the word about the orchestra."

Like many responsible nonprofit arts organizations, they did not embark on an "Oral Roberts School of Fundraising" campaign to avoid bankruptcy. Instead, they used their time in Chapter 11 wisely, despite the fact that there were no performances for an entire season.

"The truth is, performances cost more money than they take in," said Koch. That's not unusual – generally speaking, no nonprofit arts organization makes money on any performance. The cost structure, the ticket ceiling, and all the rest lead the most veteran financial managers astray in thinking that the expenses on a single performance would ever be recouped. Most lose money on every performance.

In August 2011, when they got their affairs in order enough for the judge to allow LO to emerge from bankruptcy, things had changed. The company had to be careful with its financial commitments.

"Coming back," said McSorley, "we only had a one-year contract with the musicians. We had fewer players and we had fewer weeks at that point. We went from 71 players to 55 and 42 weeks to 30 weeks."

From Chapter 11 to huge success is a long road, and in this case, is largely due to the great work that Teddy Abrams and Graham Parker have done in their quest to follow a charitable path. Each goes into the community to ask what potential partners need to improve their lives. In return, they find people who can increase the impact of LO on the millions of Kentuckians who benefit personally from their work. It is more important to Abrams and Parker to help others in need than to garner great musical acclaim. The post-bankruptcy musicians come aboard because they know about the orchestra's reputation to put others ahead of themselves. They are not corporate ghosts, but artists who just want to play, make a positive difference in the lives of those that need it, and get paid for doing so.

That being said, one of the clearest reasons why Abrams and Parker are successful in going out into the community is they never have to worry about what's going on at home. That's what Nate Koch and Tonya McSorley do. They follow the instructions on the old *Hitchhiker's Guide to the Galaxy*: "Don't panic." But neither are they grizzled veterans. In fact, their energy is as vibrant as anyone in the building. The company is fortunate to have those two in tow.

The Board: Support, Encouragement, and Zeal when It Counted

Andrew Fleischman

"I was the chair of the music director search committee," remembered Andrew Fleischman, currently the president of the board of directors (2024). "When Teddy was 24, we met him here in Louisville. He did an interview with a group of us. We took Teddy for his first bourbon. He was so young. However, the way he taught us about impact, we thought he could be our next *Executive* Director. He's, but he's always been this way. He gives us the confidence to embrace being a cultural, impactful organization. I didn't know that we could. I know we weren't that sort of organization before Teddy, and I give him most of the credit. So, we've kind of rallied around him and enabled the circumstances for it to develop. Teddy is really special."

The board, according to Fleischman, is divided among three general advocacy groups.

"Graham Parker tends to want to connect with influential people connected with the largest, most successful buzzy organizations. He reads something about somebody who has recently been appointed the new CEO of some company, and he'll notice that the leader is new to the area. Then he gravitates toward new and exciting people. He specifically looks for strong people of a diverse background, people whose ideas are not currently represented on the board."

"Then," Fleischman continued, "we've got the group who are passionate about what we do, about the means of our delivery of impact, which is classical music, and music in general. People who really love it, who've done it and feel passionate about music that we're making, and passionate about how we're doing it in the community. Then you've got a third group of people who are very well connected and who are influencers. We really want to connect with these people to use their ideas and learn everything we can about the people they represent, as part of our board."

As I attended a board meeting for the company, the familiar thrums of budget analysis, gala and other giving, and board nomination rang through the room. The meeting was quite formal in nature, and yet relaxed as well. There is a great deal of confidence in the direction of the organization's executive leadership and, while there are still some vestigial members from previous administrations that never worked as well as this one does, there doesn't seem to be a pull toward the notion that "things were better back then." Thanks to the ability to reach into the various communities of Kentucky and changing (and saving) lives, the Louisville Orchestra's board is ready for new challenges.

The first of those new challenges should probably include a deeper dive into the portions of the community in which non-Whites are not the majority population. The company has a lot of White decision-makers and knows it has to increase (and then listen to) diverse voices with power in order to make their work even more impactful.

The company itself engages in a program called Music Without Borders, a set of activities put forth to find ways (again) to bring a neighborhood's music to where they are. They perform these activities in three distinct Black neighborhoods of Louisville: California, Shelby Park, and Jeffersontown. Ostensibly, it is a set of programs that enables Metro Louisville to achieve a goal of community healing, engagement, and celebration in light of the horrors of the Breonna Taylor killing and other anti-Black attacks by providing free community concerts in traditional (and some non-traditional) gathering places such as the St. Vincent de Paul subsidized housing area, aka "The Projects." Building trust and unifying neighbors at the schools, healthcare facilities, and other community organizations in these neighborhoods is not an easy task, but music and music education programs can use a common, non-threatening language to build connections. It's a small program now but has the capacity and potential to work deeply with the residents, students, and other members of these communities. Using everything from drum circles to "Orchestral Instrument Playgrounds," from performances to community panels and discussions, and by bringing in guest artists to combine with artists who already live in these neighborhoods, the goals are deep. It is a replicable program that easily could be applied statewide in communities that are feeling the same racist issues of oppression, redlining, and inequity.

For the board to increase a worthy and singular program such as Music Without Borders, more money, more members of the neighborhoods involved, and more personnel, comprised of people in these neighborhoods, will be required. This will be a bit of a challenge, but not out of reach for an organization that has achieved greatness on a level unmatched in the United States in terms of combining great music with deep personal and community connections with the underserved in the state.

When representative of all the socioeconomic and ethnic backgrounds of the area, they'll be building an even stronger foundation than is currently in place. When equitable diversity happens in leadership, the risk of the company shifts from a small group of elites (Whites) to a larger group of community members (with diversity representative of the population), and with that shift comes a stronger case to be made for all the things that are important to a nonprofit: funding, marketing, and most importantly, need for impactful, measurable results.

Right now, one of the great strengths of the Louisville Orchestra is that it can talk about the work it has already done to increase inclusionary efforts in the commonwealth of Kentucky. Its results page is not filled with empty manifesto promises of "we will do this" or "we will do that." The LO can tell you "we did this" and "we did that" and provide compelling evidence. Companies that promise and do not deliver have far less right to crow about DEI or any other championing cause than do companies that deliver.

The life of Kentucky and the US is integral to the work of the Louisville Orchestra, not unlike the best orchestras in the world — those that embrace their culture rather than hide behind it to present a copy of how they believe a fine European orchestra might act. Authenticity is the hallmark of the LO. Like musical director Teddy Abrams and the people whose American orchestral shoulders on which he stands (Michael Tilson-Thomas, Leonard Bernstein, Aaron Copeland, Scott Joplin, etc.), the Louisville Orchestra stands as the most complete, vital, and authentically American orchestra in the world.

The Open Fifth

The perfect way to describe the culture of the region can be found in the principal feature of the music of this region, "the open fifth." In Louisville, with all that bourbon sloshing about, an open fifth might mean there's a party going on. Or, that it's, I don't know, Tuesday.

But in a musical sense, the open fifth is that bare, unfulfilling sound when the two notes DO and SOL are played together. Sometimes it is transposed to appear to be an "open fourth" when the two notes are SOL and the higher DO. But the feeling is the same either way. Whether the open fifth is performed by a choir, a bluegrass fiddle, or a symphony orchestra, it has a mischievous, reedy quality, even when played quickly. Unresolved, it offers the idea that something is afoot.

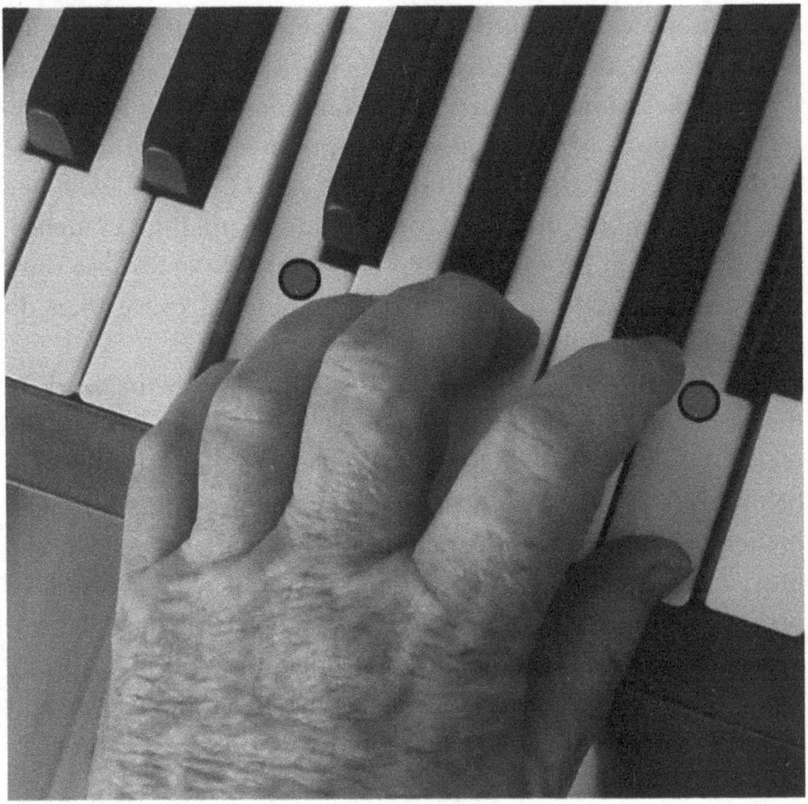

If you add a note between DO and SOL, the feeling of the music changes radically. Adding MI, for example, makes it a bright, major, birds-are-singing-and-all-is-right-with-the-world musical moment. But if you drop that third note by a half-step – ME (pronounced "meh" or "may") – the result is a dreadful, minor, sorrowful, they're-throwing-babies-from-the-balcony musical moment. The tipping point between happiness and sadness is determined by a half-step.

So, in essence, until that "open fifth" is fulfilled by a third note, the future can go either way with the slightest of change. It won't take the enormous power of a winning lottery ticket or a nuclear warhead's worth of impact to change the result. Just the placement of a little, tiny third note. By not including that note, it leaves the future open.

When the LO decided to bring its music to the people — rather than just being another good orchestra playing for rich, White people — they could have celebrated the notion by hoisting major-chord praise upon themselves. It could have been a moment of happy inclusiveness, one that required no additional support or fulfilled no other need.

But they didn't do that. Abrams refused to add that third to the chord. The "open fifth" remained intact and ready to adapt. Abrams called it a "distinctive American sound."

"I think if you look at it as a metaphor," he said, "then as we come to communities locally or throughout the state, we're not trying to tell people what to think or how to think. This is not some kind of subliminal program to get people to think about something politically. We're not trying to sneak in a hidden message through our music. We're not trying to sell people on an ideology. This really is a celebration of largely American and Kentucky music. But also music from all eras with no agenda."

"The only agenda is that we ask people to interact," he continued. "And a lot of times, maybe this speaks to what we're talking about, that the interactions need to be honest. So sometimes we are celebrating in the sense of talking about our achievements and joys, our share of accomplishments. But we also need to find unity in speaking about the really difficult things we're confronting. We're not telling people that we should just be dancing and celebrating because everything is fine. But we're also not telling people that everything is so terrible that there's no hope. Through this music, we're asking people to actually look at the totality of the human experience right now and to share that amongst each other even if we come from very different backgrounds. Not to do that in a way that distances each other. Not to do it in a way that makes people feel like they don't belong. I think that's the power of this music and maybe that's the metaphor of the open fifth. It's a house that allows us all to actually find some peace. In a way, it's a kind of modern spirituality because clearly religion doesn't provide that same national unity. But music somehow does."

"To Change Lives throughout Our Entire Community"

Connecting with the people of Kentucky by providing services where arts organizations have never been in the past is the primary goal of the company. However, Kentuckians can be made more tolerant, more open to change and cultural shifts, and more engaged – in essence, more whole – can be done through the work of the LO. The same applies to almost every region in America, and the key to success is intent. The orchestra just has to want to.

Oh, the LO isn't doing everything "right." That would be a miracle. Staff and board members alike would be the first to tell you that it's been a bumpy ride since before the height of the pandemic, 2020–2022. The path toward full civic change is as muddy and uneven as a Kentucky Derby race during a real toad-strangler (a local phrase meaning "downpour").

But it is a path worth taking because, as one staff member put it, "As long as we're here on Earth, we might as well do something to make things better for everyone else who's here."

Teddy Abrams and Graham Parker

America doesn't have just one orchestra or is part of some fictitious National Orchestra League in which there are franchises in Cleveland, New York, Los Angeles, Louisville, or San Francisco. That would be ridiculous.

As such, and this emphasis is a key to this particular success story, this is the *LO*. No other orchestra creates the powerful impact for Louisville and the rest of Kentucky. It could not exist anywhere else because these people partner with the people who live here — all the people, not just the elite.

And that's how Music Director Teddy Abrams and Chief Executive Graham Parker prefer it. That's why, unlike many of their colleagues at other first-class orchestras (including those that may not have won a Grammy®), Teddy lives in Louisville. He couldn't imagine being effective while living somewhere else.

"I think it's necessary, at least for me," said Abrams. "You have to be here to meet people. It's not just about shaking people's hands after a concert. That's not enough. It's the act of living in a place, of getting into the rhythm and flow and listening to people and spending time with them."

To hear Abrams talk about how he came to be *this* conductor at *this* orchestra at *this* time in *this* region, it evokes a series of pinball cushions that appear to be random, but are in fact resolute, defining choices that could land him nowhere else. His life might be defined in more recognizable terms as a young gymnast or skater, one whose early prowess led to more interesting paths (in all senses of the word "interesting") than the average creative force.

Talking with Teddy Abrams about the purpose of the Orchestra evokes a vision of putting a giant metal rod into an even larger electric outlet. He fairly hums with a captivating enthusiasm, all at about 100 miles an hour. But if you can listen as fast as he dreams, you'll become a fan, I promise you.

"My job," said Abrams, "is to be a public servant in Louisville. You build community by using the power of the art form to convene people."

But convening is not the beginning and end of the purpose of the company. That happens at any nonprofit arts organization as a byproduct. Any audience could be construed as a "convening." Abrams takes it further, in a city that has seen multiple challenges for its arts organizations.

"The pandemic was when this all really shifted for us, because that's when I basically said to our people that we needed to frame the institution as an essential part of the town, not as a vestigial thing that could be cut, something no one would notice. We talked about what we do as something that can be framed and structured around an essential thing that people love and care about and can't imagine living without. If we could do that, we'd be just fine. We have to stick to that, and that it would be hard to always draw from the same vision source, but we could do it.

"Many places in America have not come to terms with what American culture truly is. We're still at war with ourselves. We still want to compete with this vague notion of European artistic excellence. And that's what all these organizations are structured on. And we as an American orchestra ecosystem still have not fully recognized the value of what American culture really might be, which is crazy."

It took Teddy Abrams five years to complete community college. Don't jump to conclusions.

He started college at age eleven.

"I grew up in the San Francisco Bay Area," recalled Abrams. "In third grade, we were given the option to sign up for the elementary school band program that was just being started at my school. They brought in a band from another school for us to see what a band was and that little performance, which I'm sure sounded exactly like an elementary school band, was so amazing to us that every single kid in school signed up. I wanted to play the saxophone, but when we went to the music store to get one, they told me that my hands were too small. The staff at the music store said that the closest relative is the clarinet. 'Since you're already playing piano, you might like that, because it can play classical music and jazz,' they told me. I was more interested in jazz. When I started playing the clarinet, it came naturally to me, I still can't explain it. But within about a week, I'd finished the whole band book. I don't know why. I can't explain it. But that's the reason that my parents took me to my first concert."

Even though his parents were both cultured and intellectually gifted, the act of attending live performances was not a regular part of their schedule. His parents brought him to an all-Gershwin concert when he was nine years old, his first encounter with the San Francisco Symphony and its world-famous, talented conductor, Michael Tilson Thomas (MTT). That was the moment when Abrams decided to be a conductor. He wrote MTT a letter.

"He wrote me back," Abrams remembered with some surprise. "I asked him for conducting lessons and he gave me all kinds of amazing advice. That's when I took the clarinet really, really seriously. I started dividing my time between studying in San Francisco and New York with this legendary but overly domineering teacher. So, when I was ten, eleven, and twelve years old, I would fly back and forth from San Francisco to New York. I still wanted to be a conductor, but the clarinet took up all of my energy."

Working with a taskmaster instructor was challenging for a pre-teenage child, especially when traveling across the country to do it. It was not a good arrangement for anyone. His parents turned to the San Francisco Symphony for help, where MTT helped guide the young man's educational choices. After ending the relationship with the unruly taskmaster, Teddy Abrams graduated from elementary school and enrolled at Peralta Community College.

You know. Like you do.

"I was literally a full-time student at community college from age eleven. So I was already on this very weird path educationally. I think that's why my parents wanted advice from people that they trusted."

MTT invited the Abrams family to his house, Teddy played the clarinet, and together, all parties debated the next steps to create the best learning environment for the talented tween in the room.

"I know how crazy this all sounds. Here I am — a twelve-year-old — with MTT in his living room, poring over my music education. He set me up with a clarinet teacher, a piano teacher, and a musicianship and theory teacher. Then he said, when he was in town, I would come play for him. He'd kind of supervise and, you know, make sure that everything was going in the right direction."

After that, MTT invited Abrams to conduct the New World Symphony, even though he was still only 13 years old. Abrams came back every year, several times a season, and received conducting lessons.

16-year-old Teddy Abrams conducting the New World Symphony in 2003. Michael Tilson Thomas (upper right) looks on.

When he graduated from Peralta, he was 16. "I walked out with the equivalent of two years of college credits," he said. "So, I transferred to the San Francisco Conservatory of Music. I really bunched up my education, I did all my juries and recitals and everything else that I need to do to get a bachelor's degree in a couple of years, and that meant I could leave San Francisco as an 18-year-old, just like all my friends."

Of course, his friends were just starting college. At 18, Abrams was starting graduate school. He started attending the Curtis Institute of Music in Philadelphia. "I loved Curtis. It was such a perfect environment for me. I formed lifelong bonds with students who are remarkably gifted, and I still work with many of them on an everyday basis."

After three years at Curtis, Abrams went to the New World Symphony to work with MTT as the official Conducting Fellow. Finally, he was no longer the youngest person in the room.

Then, seemingly out of nowhere, he accepted an appointment as the conductor of a symphony in the European musical hotbed of Budapest, Hungary. "I took a position as the conductor of the MÁV Symphony Orchestra," he said, "which is one of eleven or twelve full-time professional orchestras in Budapest alone. The very first concert I did was an outdoor show of all Strauss waltzes. Strauss wrote half of those waltzes in Budapest. This was in the community's DNA, a very personal experience for most of the people in the crowd."

This is where the pinball effect bounced in exactly the right spot. Some might call Teddy lucky to have been in the right place at the right time, but all that is meaningless unless you are mentally and practically prepared for success.

"It's kind of a strange thing. I really wasn't looking for jobs," said Abrams. This is not unusual for many people — amazing things happen sometimes when you're not looking for it. "When I stopped caring about jobs or thinking about them too much, that's when things started lining up. The next year, I got the job at the Detroit Symphony Orchestra (DSO)."

Once Abrams took the job at the DSO, he heard that the LO was looking for a new music director. "I did two years at the DSO, which were also extremely formative," he recalled. "That was fascinating, because they had just come out of a strike, similar to what the Louisville Orchestra had been through. I was able to watch the process play out because the DSO was a little farther ahead.

"Between Detroit and the New World and Curtis and San Francisco, of course, being a part of the Youth Symphony growing up, I had a big spread of what leadership looked like. I saw what 'mission' looked like. I learned what it meant for an institution to drive towards a mission. As I was coming into the Louisville job — with that experience and those observations over the years — I think that's extremely important. I don't know how I could have done this job if I didn't have those models upon which to draw."

But of all the influences on his life, his mind often returns to Oakland, California, where he was raised.

"Most of my upbringing was in the East Bay. That was very influential and important. This was before the tech boom, so I could see inequalities and inequity everywhere. Even as a kid, I started teaching in Oakland Public Schools. When I graduated elementary school, I asked my band coach what I could do to help with other elementary schools, and he had a whole portfolio and some were more affluent than others. He would bring me to the ones that were really struggling. He'd ask me to help the clarinet kids, because he thought that if some of these kids saw a clarinetist who was just a little bit older than they were – if an eight-year-old saw an eleven-year-old who really could play the clarinet and took it seriously – he thought that it might help them grow confidence in themselves. That was hugely formative for me, too, as an eleven-year-old w kid talking to mostly Black and Hispanic kids from poor neighborhoods in Oakland. Sometimes, I can't even believe that I was even given that opportunity. But far more influential on me than any other thing in terms of how to teach and communicate."

This unusual upbringing thus informed Abrams's work at the LO, where the focus is not on the art, but on the community. All of his experiences combined to help him realize that fulfillment could only come with a blend of the art and the civic work for the betterment of all, no matter where they stood on the racial, ethnic, or socio-economic ladder.

"I want to contribute to the societal, functioning, and cohesion elements that have become the hallmark of our work in Louisville."

So far, so good.

Graham Parker

Graham Parker, born and raised in the outskirts of northwest London, also has enjoyed a career with exciting pinball movement, even more chaotic than Teddy Abrams. Still, like Abrams, Parker had smart parents who, while not in the music business, were part of a larger family with players here and there. He was an ambitious child that gravitated towards music at a young age. He started taking piano lessons at six. His life is peppered with magnificent accomplishments and tragic disappointments, not unlike a Steinbeck family saga or a Puccini opera.

"My grandmother on my mum's side," Parker recounted, "was very musical and could play piano by ear and did that 'Second-World-War-playing-the-front-parlor' sort of thing. Music hall songs to keep everyone singing during the air raids. I have a cousin on my mum's side who's a professional cellist. So there is music in the family, but I was always the kid that just like, you know, my parents could never understand where I got it from, why I was interested."

When he started secondary school, he started playing the flute and singing in the choir.

"You hear the story over and over about how there's a music teacher that affects your life," remembered Parker (incidentally, thank you, Eloise Haldeman). "The school I went to was a very English kind of all-boys private school. The head of music was just one of those brilliant musicians who was like a god. He went to Oxford. He was a choral and an organ scholar. We sang so much incredible repertoire. It was incredible. I really just leaned into music and thought about applying for a choral scholarship to Oxford or Cambridge."

Parker was a good singer, but not a great one. He asked for his head of music's opinion on the idea. "He said to me, 'Parker, you're good, but you're not good enough. I just want to be honest with you now because you're just going to be disappointed.' And it was just like, whoof, I guess *that's* not going to be a pathway."

Failure, as we all know now, is a guardrail, not a monolith. Failure offers paths to success, but it's hard to see that on the heels of disappointing news. As a young man, Parker was crestfallen. However, he was not without resources.

The other thing that he'd always had, and still does, is a leadership quality. Parker was always coming up with some crazy idea and making it happen. He decided to pursue a management undergraduate degree in hotel/restaurant management, mostly because he also loves to cook.

"I went to Oxford Brookes University," he said. "It's the best hotel school in the UK. But it's in Oxford. I formed a chamber choir and started conducting the orchestra. Then I started doing things at the university. I was the music director of the Oxford University Gilbert and Sullivan Society, which was a fairly awful experience, for all the reasons you might guess."

With all the extra-curricular activities, Parker's schoolwork was suffering. His parents insisted that he give up something, so he gave up the piano and continued with the flute. "Oh, that was a huge mistake, because every time I went, I tried to audition for a conducting program, they asked questions such as, 'Can you transpose the piano on the spot?' I just couldn't do it. But, put me in front of the choir, and I was really good. But without advanced training on the piano, I just couldn't do everything they asked of me."

Even with all the music, Graham Parker was still on the road to a career in hotel management.

"I ended up running a high-class Dean & DeLuca-type chain. A deli. I was using my management degree and running a business for the owner and growing it. But two times every week at lunch, I would go up to university and conduct."

Parker was determined to get to New York, with or without a conducting program, and get into the music business.

"When I told my friends that I was moving to New York," he laughed, "people asked me what I'd do when I got there. My reply was that maybe I'd get a job in marketing for the New York Philharmonic." His friends rolled their collective eyes.

At 25, he obtained a visa and moved to the US, where he got a job as a restaurant system manager. There was a mysterious job posting in *The New York Times*. "Prominent New York arts institution requires marketing assistant. Send your résumé."

Parker sent his résumé to a blind Post Office box. About a week later, the New York Philharmonic called him. And yes, it was for a job in marketing.

"I went in for an interview and I think they could not make head nor tail of me. You look at my résumé, and there's hotel restaurant management, but I'd done all this conducting as well. I hadn't done the thing that a lot of kids would do — an undergraduate performing arts degree, a master's in marketing, or any of that. But once I got the job, I asked my boss, 'Lois, why did you choose me?' And she said, 'I couldn't understand a word you said. Your accent was so strong. I just saw Oxford at the bottom of your résumé and that was enough for me.'"

But Parker proved his mettle, his worth, and something more — resilient ambition.

"I went to work at the New York Philharmonic in 1995. Deborah Borda was the executive director. Kurt Masur was the music director. Catherine Cahill was the general manager, and Lois Cohn, who was my big boss, was a very famous publicist in New York. Lois ran marketing and PR. There was also a famous tension between Masur and Deborah. I was in the marketing and PR department, just drinking from a fire hose of learning. I stayed in marketing for about three years."

A 25-year-old Graham Parker at the NY Philharmonic, pictured here with his then-intern, Sharon Lu

"Deborah took a real shine to me," remembered Parker. "She mentored me. She asked me, in no uncertain terms, what I wanted to be when I grew up. 'I think you're smart, you're very good. Everyone likes you.' I told her that essentially, I wanted to be her. She advised me to get out of marketing and get into artistic administration or general management, because that's generally the way to be an executive director. At her suggestion, I applied for an opening in the operations department at the Phil. I got to work much more closely with Masur and help with the radio broadcasts. It was my first chance to build relationships with artists."

Graham knew he'd hit a ceiling at the New York Philharmonic. Following his mentor's advice, he took a job with the Chamber

Music Society of Lincoln Center (CMS) as their director of production. "At that time, there was an extraordinary executive director there called Jacqueline Taylor. She's still an extremely close friend and a massive mentor of mine and she was running the CMS with David Shifrin."

"We did the first ever free Beethoven cycle of string quartets at Lincoln Center with the Orion String Quartet. That would have been remarkable all by itself, but the way Jackie brilliantly conceived it, it was done all with community groups giving away the tickets (not us), and we enjoyed the most diverse and appreciative audience you've ever seen in your life for Beethoven String Quartets. It was packed."

Then there was a program that cellist Fred Sherry conceived, called *Great Day in New York,* which was modeled after a famous photo taken in Harlem in 1958 of all the jazz greats of the time sitting on a stoop. Sherry conceived the idea that he could do a series of performances with 100 great New York-based living composers. Parker produced all nine concerts.

Again, after Jackie Taylor left, he hit another ceiling.

Parker took the job as the general manager of the struggling Brooklyn Philharmonic. A great job at a struggling arts organization is risky. One never knows whether the sickness is fatal or curable. (More often than not, it's fatal.) The leaders *at the time of closure* are the ones who get blamed for the death even though they were not the ones who dished out the poison, which can cause even the most burgeoning career to stagger. But there are other reasons to take a difficult job, especially when an organization's figurative back is against the wall, and Parker knew that.

"It was kind of a mess. But someone said to me, 'the reason you should take this job is to work with [music director] Robert

Spano.' And then we went through September 11 together and I programmed the Brooklyn Memorial Concert at the Brooklyn Academy of Music (BAM). It was very powerful."

But not for long. After only 18 months, Parker took a newly created opportunity at the Orpheus Chamber Music Ensemble, a strong mainstay in the field, but another company suffering financial pains of its own.

There had been some alleged financial shenanigans executed by the previous executive director just to enable cash flow. Money had been siphoned off from federal payroll taxes, it was believed, in order to pay current vendors, a typical trick played by unscrupulous and desperately bad leadership.

"It was horrendous," Parker remembered with a shudder. "They could have shut us down. I mean, we got it all figured out, but it took a number of years. We rebuilt the board, changed the staff, and started building the artistic credibility of Orpheus because the word on the street was that there were some artistic issues. We started a brand-new commissioning program. We got back on the radio. I got them a new record contract.

"I did Orpheus for eight years, which was incredible. I loved it."

But the pinball bounced off yet another cushion, landing Parker an unusually remarkable opportunity only available in New York.

Out of nowhere, WQXR called. WQXR was (and still might be) the national leader for classical music radio. They needed a new general manager to run the station. "I reminded them that I'd never run a radio station before, to which they responded that they didn't want someone who'd run a radio station. 'You've got a great network. You know how to raise money. Everyone in the artist community seems to know you.' They asked me to conceive – *reconceive* – WQXR. It'd have been sold by [its previous owners] *The New York*

Times a couple of years earlier and had to transform quickly to a non-profit, classical public radio station. They needed to build a membership base, a donor base, a web presence, and they had to quickly learn about streaming online. The digital profile of QXR had to be completely reimagined with a number of programming changes. I loved it. I did it for six years."

Then, again out of nowhere, he got a call from Universal Music Group. They asked him to run all their record labels – Decca, Deutsche Grammaphon, UCM – in America. He considered not taking the job, until "UMG sweetened the pot: they wanted me to start an A&R [artists and repertoire] center, their first in the United States. And the big one: they wanted me to start my own label."

"I was thinking about what my vision would be for that label and I was thinking of American artists that push the boundary of music and society."

And then he met Teddy Abrams. At 27, Abrams was very clear about his vision for the city, for the LO, and all the work he'd done to achieve some form of greatness. Parker was intrigued and flew to Louisville.

"I heard the orchestra and was blown away. I immediately signed them to a record deal. We did two records together. Then I signed Teddy to a record as a solo artist, a pianist/composer. Then during the pandemic, we got very close and chatted a lot and started to understand more and more about his sociopolitical and musical kind of intersections."

When Parker left UMG, he knew when the artists on his roster were going to be told that he was leaving the company. Teddy Abrams waited three minutes and called Parker. "And he was generally concerned about me and asked how I was doing. I told him that my immediate plans were to do some consulting. He asked me, 'Would you consider helping us out in Louisville?'"

Graham and Teddy, I believe this is the beginning of a beautiful friendship. (Photo from "Casablanca," public domain)

"Of all the things that I learned in my career, the most important is that when you have a partnership with someone on the artistic side — and Teddy isn't just an artistic guide, he's an institutional guide — when you have a mind-meld about the potential of what you could change, deliver, affect people, communities, policy, life, and joy and happiness, I knew that for the rest of my career, I want to do that. So, we explored how we could make that happen."

Parker told me why the LO was interested. "Teddy told me that I was the first partner he'd ever had in this orchestra who totally understands the big idea here. My whole career has always been about this kind of intersection of impact of music. So I said, 'Let's do this.' I'm now into yet another year, and everyone seems to be pretty happy."

"It's rough. It's really rough," he sighed. "Every arts organization in Louisville has been through the wringer. Nobody's had a sustained, steady, couple decades of growth.

Every single one of them has some scandal, some financial meltdown. It's just bad for the art. It's bad for the confidence in these institutions."

When existential threats threaten the very existence of a nonprofit arts organization (and many others as well), that organization often starts losing its sense of purpose and engages in "mission creep." Its once-stalwart mission drifts toward the garnering of cash, which leads to a constancy of disaster mode. Big vision gets sacrificed for survival, which in turn is sacrificed for short-term financial bailout. What really gets sacrificed, of course, is the community services it requires to increase its citizens' quality of life. That makes the public lose confidence. Ultimately, that's what kills the arts nonprofit.

When the arts nonprofit — like the Louisville Orchestra — measures its value as an organization by the integration of good works to its underserved (or often unserved) taxpaying community members, it has the potential to be indispensable. Indispensability keeps organizations vital, not someone's version of excellence. Indispensability allows communities of people, people who would never set foot in an orchestra hall, to step-dancing in the aisles to a bluegrass/orchestral music combination at a high school gym, not "artistic vision."

In Harmony: It's Not Just About Great Music

The LO embarked on a two-year statewide tour of Kentucky called "In Harmony," the revenue for which came in large part by the state. It was so successful, it was renewed for two more years, thanks to two things. First, the people of the LO believe that their nonprofit orchestra, being owned by the state that granted its ability to be exempt from some taxes, has a duty to its owners. As such, while they are relatively agnostic to how other arts organizations handle their affairs, the LO believes — stridently, determinedly, vociferously, enthusiastically, and correctly — that their mission enhances the education and the culture of thousands of non-Louisvillian Kentuckians through the power of the meshing of local and symphonic music. It is an orchestra that could only exist and thrive in Kentucky. Its strength as an organization lies in that focus and, while excellence is subjective and not the goal, its music has proof of excellence denoted by awards, record sales, and glowing artistic reviews.

Second, while touring, they could merely do evening performances at other sites and call it a day. Instead, they *choose* to do the hard work of unifying forgotten people in the arts world in order to keep it from drowning in the industry's current whirlpool of elitism and toxicity.

Both reasons speak to the commonwealth's decision to fund the program. Rural taxpayers benefitted from these tours. So did urban taxpayers.

If there's an important conversation between someone who primarily speaks Ukrainian and someone who primarily speaks English, not much will happen until you find a common denominator. Only when we bother to discover that each has some fluency in French can the conversation really take place. Such is the music of Kentucky, as it relates to both rural folks and city dwellers. This particular program, In Harmony, combines the music of the region with a first-class symphony orchestra.

> *Music makes me feel better about the world. Music has brought me this new aspect in the way of seeing things in life. Music's cool. It's very cool. If you can play an instrument, you can do things that other people cannot do. And you can understand things that other people cannot understand.*
>
> *— Kentucky High School Senior and Tuba Player*

On February 28, 2024, on the floor of the Kentucky state senate, Senator Gerald A. Neal talked about why music — and the work of the Louisville Orchestra, which transcends music —

can change the world for so many people in his life. In response to a vote on the floor to issue a resolution honoring the LO for winning a Grammy® Award, Senator Neal talked about his own family's attachment to music, not merely as an art form, but as a language to bridge the generations and heal families.

"I have to tell you that my father made sure that all of his children played musical instruments. So I grew up on clarinet. So I made sure all my kids played musical instruments. And my son, although I sent him to middle school with a saxophone, he came back with a tuba.

"I didn't know at the time, although I was disappointed we spent all that money, that he was going to perfect his act with the tuba. And he ended up traveling through Europe with that tuba with a young orchestra and adult supervision.

"So they come back and I'm trying to make my son a lawyer, he ends up saying, 'No, I'm doing music.' I said, 'No, you're not doing music. You're doing law.' He says, 'No, I'm doing music.' He ends up saying, 'Dad, please support me.' He knew how to get to me, right? So he goes to music school at University of Louisville. I didn't know until two years later that the person who supervised them in Europe was the dean of the music school from the University of Louisville. I did not have a chance.

"He's now a producer in the Office of the President at Juilliard in New York City. So you don't know what happens when you open up the world of music. I know it because I embraced it so readily and I'm sure the members here as well.

"But when I look at the Louisville Orchestra ... Man, I change my plans! I've got to find out where they are! Because they are stellar. They are the top, top of the game!

"I think this resolution is a great tribute from the Senate in acknowledging their value and the value of music and the power, the power you provide young people when they are trying to navigate life and acquire those attributes that you guys display so readily. God bless you."

"I Can See the Change That We're Trying to Make Actually Happening"

From September 2024, through May 2025, the LO scheduled seventeen traditional, just-like-every-other-orchestra performances in their main symphony space, the 2,377-seat Whitney Hall (named for the Orchestra's former conductor, Robert Whitney), which is part of the Kentucky Center for the Performing Arts, which opened in 1983. They scheduled six performances at the 2,800-seat Louisville Palace, a Broadway touring house built in 1928. The 500-seat Stem Concert Hall at the Ogle Center, on the campus of Indiana University Southeast (New Albany, Indiana, about 11 miles from Whitney Hall) is the home for four more performances.

"Performances can cost about $100,000 apiece at Whitney Hall," said one staff member, "and while it's a lovely venue and load-in and load-out couldn't be easier, it's imposing as hell to anyone coming to a concert for the first time."

Designed by Caudill, Rowlett & Scott, an architectural firm from Houston, the Kentucky Center for the Arts represented the fortress/prison/university style of civic design popular in the 1980s. It was meant to be striking, not welcoming, and it has achieved that objective. It is a pristine building with horizontal lines and curves, sharp angles, and multitudinous large panes of glass. A modern performance center in downtown Louisville, where many buildings are over 100 years old, the Kentucky Center for the Performing Arts was a design of its time but intimidates too many who have never been inside.

Western Hills High School in Frankfort, Kentucky, was ranked #7,497 among 17,655 public high schools in the United States by *US News and World Report*. It is ranked #103 among high schools in the state of Kentucky. Of its student body, 45% are financially disadvantaged and receive free or reduced-price meals and 23% are non-White. Opened in 1979, the school's domed gymnasium hosts Wolverine basketball and other arena sports. That gym housed an In Harmony performance of the Louisville Orchestra, who played with bluegrass Grammy® winners Michael Cleveland and Flamekeeper.

Needless to say, the gym intimidates no one. Except, maybe, sound engineers and opposing basketball teams.

The acoustics were live, to say the least. Hard surfaces throughout. Metal and plastic benches in the bleachers and a huge domed ceiling for increased echo effects — these may increase intensity and spirit for a Wolverines basketball game, but it could encourage an award-winning orchestra to seek out a more acoustically proper environment to play.

But, when your purpose as a nonprofit is to provide art as a tool to make a community better off, you don't care so much about acoustics and perfection. You care that the music — *Kentucky's* music — travels to Kentuckians. You care that the lives you touch need the encouragement and the skills attached to the making of music. You care about the community in an old-fashioned but time-proven way, that its strength emanates from coming together, not engaging in invisible arguments in social media or falling into the trap of being pitted against one another. Music can serve — and in the case of the Louisville Orchestra, *does* serve — as the common language of those who may not agree on anything else. It gives people the chance to put away binary grievances and enjoy each other's company in celebration of their own music. That's why the commonwealth of Kentucky put its financial stamp of approval on In Harmony.

"The remarkable impact of the Louisville Orchestra's 'In Harmony' tour plays a significant role in bridging the rural-urban divide," said GOP State Senator Robert Stivers, the Senate President, on the day the funding was signed into law. "This initiative extends beyond entertainment; it is a vehicle for education, cultural enrichment, and community cohesion. By supporting the continuation of this tour, we are investing in the cultural wealth of our commonwealth, reinforcing our commitment to enhancing the lives of Kentuckians through the arts. It's initiatives like these that showcase the Bluegrass State's rich artistic heritage and pave the way for a future where everyone can participate and draw inspiration in the beauty of orchestral music."

House Speaker David Osborne remarked, "The continued success of 'In Harmony – The Commonwealth Tour' represents a unique investment in our state's culture, improving quality of life and enriching our communities. The Louisville Orchestra's initiative is a testament to the power of the arts in bringing Kentuckians together and reminding us that we have a great deal to take pride in and celebrate. We are pleased to allocate funding that will not only extend this valuable program but also amplify its reach to more communities, ensuring that every Kentuckian has the opportunity to experience this incredible asset to our Commonwealth."

Community leaders and audience members have expressed their profound appreciation for the tour's impact. Gwen Johnson, Director of the Hemphill Community Center, shared, "Our somewhat forgotten community was encouraged to believe that someone cares enough to bring their talent to us. The concert was a 'classical first-ever' experience for us in our community." These testimonials reinforce the significance of the Orchestra's mission to bring music to diverse audiences.

Candid photos from West Hills High School, Frankfort, KY, from the In Harmony tour

When your goal is to create a better community using art as a tool, and not as a product, your influence and impact becomes far greater than some convoluted search for excellence.

"Artistic excellence is not a result. It's a practice," recounted Teddy Abrams about what matters for an impactful nonprofit arts organization. "Your company should be artistically excellent anyway. Who doesn't want to be artistic? Who goes in saying, 'We're going to do the community engagement thing, but now we're not going to be artistically excellent.' And it's certainly not a result of a mission. You shouldn't say if everything goes well, it will be artistically excellent. That's insane, that doesn't mean anything at all, that's just words thrown together."

The Louisville Orchestra saves lives. Not in a metaphorical way. In the real way.

I get straight As and I'm in a few AP courses, too. But I was lost, depressed, my home life was a bust, and I didn't see that I had any future. Then I saw the Louisville Orchestra last year and started a love of music. I joined Band. It's the one class I can't wait to go to. Music keeps me sane. If it weren't for events like this with the Louisville Orchestra, and I know this sounds pretty dark, I probably would be dead. I've been through a bunch of suicidal ideations in the past, but I learned that music is the one thing I'm very good at in this world. Having the opportunity to see great music here at my own high school lets me know I have a future.

— Student in attendance at an In Harmony concert

The previous paragraph was from one interview in one school in one city in one relatively small state. But if you were to cynically conclude that she was the only one whose magnificent life was saved by the Louisville Orchestra, think again.

In the back of a band classroom at a high school, I asked Victoria Cabral, an educator and mentor, about the power of music and its ability to downregulate teenage anxiety.

"Honestly, I hear stuff like [teen suicidal ideation] all the time. Kids talk to me. The kids will just start talking about something and then all of a sudden, somebody will just outright say, 'Well, I'm going to kill myself.' And then the other kids will slough it off by saying, 'Ah, they're just joking. They always say that.'

"And that's when I just keep listening. I'll see their mood kind of change, or I won't. But it's still a question: why would they say that? So I'll find myself talking, and then casually kind of bring it up. 'Why would you say something like that? You can't joke like that.' And then sometimes they'll say back to me, 'Oh, it wasn't really a joke. I really feel this way.' After that, they'll just start talking. They feel open enough for some reason.

"Then I'll talk to them again and ask them about programs like this one. I'll ask, 'How do you feel when you're listening to music? How do you feel when you play music?' I'll never forget this one student whose demeanor changed on the spot. She brightened up and told me that music was euphoric. That was the word she used. I told her, 'Well, that's what you need to lean on. Lean on that feeling because you don't have to deal with the bad stuff forever. It's going to go by at some point. You just need to know that.'

"Music is the most inspirational force when you can connect with it, because it can get you out of a bad day. It can help you find yourself. If you're a kid, and you're just unsure of yourself, when you start listening to different types of music, then you discover yourself. And I feel like that's so huge, because when kids aren't able to connect with other kids, or they're struggling at home, or struggling in their community, it gives them something to do. They feel better about themselves. They feel like they have found their place. And that's so important that this orchestra has brought music of all kinds to us, and by 'us,' I mean all of us. These days, we all need that kind of support.

"As for me, I have Multiple Sclerosis. I don't know what that means, but I'm guessing my time as a functioning adult is growing short. Maybe it's because of that or maybe it's just because I have teenage kids of my own, but the Louisville Orchestra is a godsend. So many kids are just so much better off because of the care the orchestra provides for them."

In Harmony concert, Western Hills High School, Frankfort, KY

"Once Upon an Orchestra," "MakingMUSIC," and Impacting Children's Futures with Art

Sarah Lempke O'Hare, the Orchestra's director of education and community partnerships, does not come from a music-first background. Her passions lie with partnerships in the community and how to make her city a wholly better place to live with the programs she helps to create, develop, and put on their respective feet.

It doesn't stop there. For what good is a program without results that show impact? As we discussed earlier, they have a data trail to measure how many people are afforded the opportunity to gain musical knowledge — free of charge, of course.

"It's been unbelievable to see the impact of the hundreds of thousands of people we have reached," said O'Hare when talking about the Orchestra's state-wide "In Harmony" tour that focuses on community engagement programs and performances in addition to full orchestra concerts.

Sarah Lempke O'Hare

"When we go into a library and do our 'Once Upon an Orchestra' program and 15 people show up we fret for a minute that that's not a very big turnout. Then we discover that 15 people might be 10% of the population of the town," she sighed.

"The feedback that we're getting from around the state has just been unbelievable. Again, it's the access piece. It's showing up in their town halls. It's showing up in their community kitchens. It's showing up in their schools and hearing students and teachers alike saying, 'I've never seen a conductor before.'"

"Once Upon an Orchestra" is a LO program that started in partnership with the Louisville Free Public Library system. The orchestra's musicians take children's stories and put them to musical programs composed by resident composers in the Creators Corps program, which we'll discuss in the next section.

The program provides a performance at every single library branch in the county, all 17 branches.

"The whole idea is about access," said O'Hare. "So many of the branches in Louisville have way more resources than others. That's just not what we believe, we want to make sure everyone has access to this. Now it's in its third year, we just got a starter grant to redo the program in alignment with kindergarten readiness literacy concepts."

I didn't know the Louisville Orchestra existed until I came to see them. Without them, I think there would be a lack of music in the schools. I mean, it would completely depend on the interest of the local teachers in elementary school, middle school, or high school. And that would adversely affect the kids at all levels. I sing in the choir, and music is something that has connected me to other people. It influences the way I dress. It influences the way I think about the whole world. It connects me to culture and to parts of myself that I didn't know existed.

— Mother and Daughter before an In Harmony concert

O'Hare and her team in partnerships collect and act upon the conclusions of a lot of fresh data, without which the program, at least to O'Hare, would be unsuccessful. She wants the music to help the youngest, most impressionable, and most vulnerable kids as well.

"We're working with the researchers out of the University of Louisville now to measure the impact primarily for pre-K kids," said O'Hare. "We're working on those programs combined with professional development of preschool teachers and how together, we can utilize music in their room to support literacy in all low-income neighborhoods."

"There's a lot of research," she continued, "about the impact of how music in particular can help kids remember, particularly story sequencing. That's what we're going to be measuring. In the study, the classes are going to be their own control and treatment where we're going to be reading books aloud without music and measuring how kids are remembering the sequence of that story."

It is the difference in comprehension between remembering the words to "Mary Had a Little Lamb" and singing the song. The latter is easier because of the musical sequencing attached to it.

"We have this really incredible resource that could support the change that any public-facing organization is trying to make in the community, whether that's a school or social service organization. So, the idea is how can we work together as partners to elevate that social service," said O'Hare.

The longest running LO community program, MakingMUSIC, has been around for more than 80 years. MakingMUSIC is about direct interactions between LO musicians and fourth- and fifth-graders in Louisville's public school system, Jefferson County Public Schools (JCPS). While it might sound a little like Leonard Bernstein's famous Young People's Concerts on CBS, it predates Lenny's television show by a fair bit.

"Right now, MakingMUSIC interacts with every fourth- and fifth-grader in the JCPS school system, and that consists of 91 elementary schools — all the schools in the JCPS," said O'Hare.

"Half of the elementary students in the fourth and fifth grade get a musician visit to their classroom. There, those musicians talk about basic music education concepts, very one-on-one. The students learn that musicians are people too, and then get an opportunity to learn about each instrument and what it's like being a musician in an orchestra."

"The other half of the elementary schools," she continued, "attend the full orchestra concerts — that's 7,500 kids in 3 days for 6 concerts. Essentially, every fourth and fifth grader will get two different experiences with the Orchestra: a musician in their classroom and then coming to see a concert."

Attending a MakingMUSIC performance brings old kids' television shows to mind. Accompanied by a group scream not unlike that heard on *Wonderama, Bozo the Clown,* and *The Winchell-Mahoney Time,* a conductor walks commandingly onto the Whitney Hall stage, picks up a microphone, and simply says, "Well, hi everybody!" to which over 2,000 children shout "Hi!" at the top of their lungs.

"It's been a founding part of this orchestra. The impact that kids get firsthand experience of what an orchestra performance is and the power that it can have on a person," said O'Hare.

O'Hare doesn't hide her pride and thanks for the progressive minds at the school district, a district that, like most, continues to see funding drop as the need for service grows.

"I am so proud of our school district and that they really value music education. The school program has a significant impact."

It's something very *Louisville* to anyone who grew up there.

"You could probably ask every board member their favorite thing about the LO. At least half of them would say coming to MakingMUSIC when they were a kid. You can walk up to any local in town and they'll tell you that they remember coming to the orchestra when they were a kid in Louisville. It's not like that in any other town in this country. It is absolutely remarkable."

Within MakingMUSIC, there are subprograms. For instance, any elementary school that brings a group of kids can nominate one of the kids attending the concert to get a conducting lesson with Teddy Abrams. Then during the concerts, they get to come up and conduct the orchestra for a small portion of time.

There is also a "Rap School" where the LO partners with Hip-Hop N 2 Learning, a nonprofit founded to provide African-American youth and young adults a platform to use hip hop, music videos, and travel to make positive changes locally, statewide, federally, and globally, helping that organization maximize its partnerships within the Louisville community doing integral, transformative work.

"And then," O'Hare added excitedly, "JCPS helped contribute to a composition program where we brought in a former Creators Corps composer to teach kids over a series of eight sessions to write their own pieces. Those compositions get performed at the MakingMUSIC concerts."

He spends his free time writing and composing music at home, and not on video games or watching TV. He's doing it on his own. Music speaks to him in a way that nothing else does. It helps him communicate fully to a wider audience. There's potentially a connection between the music and getting all As. It seems to be the same as learning another language.

— Father of a composer chosen to have his piece performed at a MakingMUSIC concert

---

"For the kids from lower income neighborhoods," O'Hare continued, "we provide extra musician visits, extra family programming, and we make sure that everyone has access to the services of this orchestra."

"I can see the change that we're trying to make actually happening," she concluded, "and that's why I love the work we do here at the Louisville Orchestra."

If a charity is an organization with philanthropic goals that aim to improve the quality of life for its community, nonprofit arts organizations have woefully underachieved. As stated earlier, intent is the number one attribute for success. When a nonprofit arts organization a) *intends* to make life better for its constituents, and b) recognizes that its constituents are not the equivalent to its audience or benefactors, but instead are comprised of those who have no resources to take advantage of the tools available to those who participate in the arts, it will succeed. The Louisville Orchestra is such an organization. Still dependent financially on donors to achieve its community goals, it serves as a mentor, as a teacher, and as a resource that engages people in order to improve their lot in life. The finances are important, and in a perfect world, several people will lay million-dollar donations at their feet, but more important is the measurable impact.

Saving people is only a start. Developing them is the ongoing mission.

"These people know what they're doing," said Rachael Boyd, a librarian in Danville, Kentucky (a college town — Centre College — about 82 miles southeast of Louisville), just after a Once Upon an Orchestra performance using the children's bestseller *Llama Destroys the World*, by Jonathan Stutzman. The reading of the story captivated over 100 people in the basement of the public library, accompanied as it was by live performances as dissimilar as *O Fortuna* from *Carmina Burana* and Usher's *Yeah!* (among others). "And they're bringing something that seems unattainable to people who might never, ever go to an orchestra performance. They're bringing it to a public place, a library — and libraries are for everybody. Anyone can walk in here, free of charge, and experience something like that? It's such a gift, a real way to improve the lives of the kids who live here."

People in small towns are more starved for the arts than the abundance of riches in larger cities. The arts are a big part of community spirit. There is town pride involved in it.

It changes the way you think. It expands your life. And it broadens your horizons significantly. At its best, programs like this transport you a bit. And if you're struggling in life and, you know, your economics aren't good or parts of your life aren't great – if you can be transported for a while, that's beautiful.

— A couple having attended a Once Upon an Orchestra event with their grandchildren at the Danville Public Library

---

And, in Case You Were Wondering, the Music Is Indeed Great

Let's get beyond the Grammy® for a moment. Lots of orchestras have won Grammy® Awards over the years. But let's take note of the backstage presser that happened right after the award was presented. This is what Teddy Abrams had to say, off the cuff, about the power of the Louisville Orchestra and its purpose for the people of Kentucky:

"We partnered with the Kentucky General Assembly, which is the state legislature, to embark on a very ambitious touring program that would bring the Louisville Orchestra to virtually every single part of Kentucky. The idea would be that we would bridge the rural/urban divide and find commonality through the language of music, using the power of the orchestra. Kentucky is famous for its musical heritage. It's a place where some of the greatest music and the greatest of American culture is derived. And so it made so much sense for the orchestra to go and not only bring music, but bring people – literally bring people together in every single part of a state that has many different backgrounds and demographics. This recording is hopefully a demonstration of the kind of extraordinary talent that's represented in our state. We're doing it on a grass-roots level, meeting people where they are, and building a much stronger Kentucky, which we hope is a model for the entire nation."

Music does not come from the ether. It comes from inspiration. It comes from talent. It comes from people.

Whether music is written down properly, improvised, accidental, or derived from jackhammers, old tapes run backwards, and car crashes (like the *musique concrète* street sounds of the cut from The Beatles's *White Album,* "Revolution 9"), it is composed. All music is composed. The key to great music is to uncover the great composers and give them the time and drive to create new ways to change the world through music.

The Louisville Orchestra does that through its Creators Corps program. Jacob Gotlib, the program's manager, and LO's most energized advocate for its adventures in new music, explained that this particular program differs from what many orchestras do. It insists on its composers living with the orchestra in Louisville to pull sounds from the state's huge musical influence, as described earlier by Abrams.

Jacob Gotlib

"The Creators Corps is a novel concept to the idea of a composer residency," said Gotlib. "Usually, the organization is in one place and the composer is somewhere else. Our approach is a very literal one. We select three composers who must live in this city over the course of a season. Not only do they live here, but they are inside of the organization. They're staff members. They are inside the building, inside the company, and part of the day-to-day process. All the people here are their colleagues or coworkers, including the musicians in the orchestra and the administrative staff. No better, no worse than anyone else."

The Creators Corps gives composers a much closer, intimate, and, ultimately, a much more fulfilling relationship with the organization than they would in a conventional composer-in-residence model. They get a salary (instead of a commission), they're each provided a separate rental house for the season, and they get health insurance through the organization. LO believes wholeheartedly that their experience living in Louisville and being part of the community informs and sharpens the work.

Gotlib believes that the composers for a Louisville Orchestra have to have Kentucky in mind as they create. Kentucky culture, its racially and socioeconomically diverse demography, and its singular attitude toward the music of its people — all its people — has to be taken into account to create great music that serves Kentuckians. Empirically great music is not enough. It has to be for Kentucky for it to achieve what the LO has in mind.

The music is dynamic, contemporary, and bespeaks the lives of the people of the commonwealth in ways that cannot be adequately described as words on a page. It has to be experienced, and it is, by numerous grateful citizens in all economic classes.

"The kinds of composers that we look for must be artistically adept and technically proficient," said Gotlib. "They have to know their way around an orchestra and have a compelling creative voice. They have to have the unique ability to think and speak about the work. But they have to also see themselves as being community-minded. They have to be interested in working with the community and producing art with and for the community. Not all composers are this way, and that's okay, there's room for every artist. However, the particular artists for whom *we* look have the same kind of mindset that resonates with the mission."

Some might ask if this wholly community-facing mission diminishes the quality of the music. In Gotlib's (and the LO's collective) mind, the quality is *because* of the connection, not in spite of it. Later, after hearing about the way the LO saved the life of the aforementioned young woman with suicidal ideations, Gotlib's eyes welled up.

"You know, working on a day-to-day basis, you work on the things that you have to do, but you can never really get many chances to zoom out and really see the impact that you have on people," he said. "When you hear something like this, then you know that what you're doing is right. You know you're heading in the right direction. It's so easy to have doubts when you're doing things that are new, like creating new work with the people of Kentucky at front-of-mind. It can be very difficult to know if you're heading in the right direction. Something like this tells me that we definitely are."

But is the music any good? Or is it just a mundane city orchestra that depends solely on community service to prove its worth?

There seems to be a binary thought process among arts leaders about the purpose of art that leads to a mythical fork in an imaginary road. Does the company seek excellence? Or does it seek community impact? Absurdly, American orchestras (and other arts organizations) default to a path of artistic excellence. Whether that's to prove some personal worth on the part of the music director (vanity) or job appointment justification for on behalf of a naïve board of directors (that has never seen its charity as anything but a performance organization that they can show off to others), too many leaders have chosen "excellence." In my research, I have found no company that solely chooses the latter path, that of community impact with no artistic effort.

Strangely, there is no conflict in choosing both paths. It is not a fork in the road at all. Choosing "excellence" (put in quotes because it's a completely subjective term and therefore meaningless) has the aphrodisiacal lure of building a better résumé. That résumé would lead to a "better" job at a bigger (higher paying) orchestra. Which leads to a "better" job at a still bigger (still higher paying) orchestra. Which leads to acting as the musical director for half a dozen orchestras around the world (more pay there, of course). Which leads to glory, ticker-tape parades, hero-worship from the press and public, knighthoods, beatification, and ultimately sainthood.

Or something like that.

The truth is that excellence makes the tool of art sharper in its use as a tool to improve the lives of the people of a community. The feeling goes well beyond what most orchestra leaders believe — that their particular production of music is good for kids (the debunked medicine argument), provides job and tax revenues (the debunked economic impact argument), and is for those that appreciate it (the hidden racist, elitist argument which never did hold water for a charitable organization like a nonprofit orchestra).

In the case of the Louisville Orchestra, the map couldn't be clearer. They do it all. Rave reviews in *The New Yorker*, *The New York Times*, and national NPR and PBS broadcasts have highlighted the company's determination to serve its people, not just by playing its great music, but by bringing it to where the people are.

And, without the full support and discipline to keep to its American roots, its Kentucky roots, its Louisville roots, it might well have become just another mundane city orchestra. It might even have produced sensational music for an audience of donors, as so many do.

Instead, the people behind this orchestra see themselves as guests in the community who have come to make a good party better (rather than being the continual "life of the party"). The LO wants to give their hosts everything they want and need. After all, these are the people not only for whom they play, but also the people who pay the LO's taxes. The community owns the company and the LO just wants to serve the owners in the best possible way. It's a good deal. The people in Kentucky, more and more each visit, get to take part in the LO instead of just listening to it.

So, while the staff list in the next section consists of the people who are on the payroll or on the board, so to speak, the Louisville Orchestra's company list ought to have at least 4,540,745 names on it – the population of the commonwealth of Kentucky as of this writing.

Author's note: On February 28, 2025, Graham Parker exited his role at the Louisville Orchestra to spend more time with his family in New York. "Careers have contours created by impact, experiences and results. This builds to create a lasting legacy and reputation....I have stepped away as full time CEO of the Louisville Orchestra to return as a consultant for the LO, focusing on fundraising and artistic planning. Working with Teddy Abrams, the Board, Orchestra and Staff in this new role will allow me to hone my energies where they are needed most right now, and spend less time away from New York City."

Just the Facts: The Louisville Orchestra

Mission Statement

"Change lives throughout our entire community as only The Louisville Orchestra can — by promoting a culture of music through outstanding performances & education."

Tax Return

For the latest tax return, visit https://apps.irs.gov/app/eos/. Under "Search By," enter "Employer Identification Number (EIN)" and under "Search Term," enter 61-6000384. Or you can always ask for a copy directly from the company. Please check the laws in your state and the state of Kentucky if you have questions.

Musicians and Staff (as of May 2024)
Teddy Abrams, Music Director
Graham Parker, Chief Executive

Bob Bernhardt, Principal Pops Conductor
Gabriel Lefkowitz, Resident Conductor

First Violin
Gabriel Lefkowitz, Concertmaster/Resident Conductor
Julia Noone, Associate Concertmaster
James Mcfadden-Talbot, Assistant Concertmaster/Acting Associate (Mrs. John H. Clay Chair)
Dillon Welch, Acting Assistant Concertmaster
Katheryn S. Ohkubo
Stephen Taylor
Scott Staidle
Nancy Staidle
Heather Thomas
Kevin Murphy, Interim

Patricia Fong-Edwards
Sabrina Parry, Interim

Second Violin
Minglun Liu, Interim Principal (Lg&E-Ku Foundation Chair)
Kimberly Tichenor
Christopher Robinson, Interim (Mary Catherine Klan Chair)
Andrea Daigle
Luis Salazar, Interim
Charles Brestel
Diane Yang, Interim
Blaise Poth

Viola
Jack Griffin, Principal
Evan Vicic, Assistant Principal/Acting Principal (Jacqueline R. and Theodore S. Rosky Chair)
Clara Markham (Mr. and Mrs. Charles W. Hebel, Jr. Chair)
Jennifer Shackleton
Jonathan Mueller (Virginia Kershner Schneider Viola Chair, Endowed in Honor Of Emilie Strong Smith By An Anonymous Donor)
Meghan Casper

Cello
Nicholas Finch, Principal (Jim & Marianne Welch Chair)
Jessamyn Fry, Interim Principal
Lillian Pettitt, Assistant Principal (Carole C. Birkhead Chair, Endowed by Dr. Ben M. Birkhead)
Cecilia Huerta-Lauf, Interim (James B. Smith Chair, Endowed by Susannah S. Onwood)
Allison B. Olsen
Lindy Tsai
Gabriel Ramos

Bass
Brian Thacker, Interim Principal
Bennett Norris, Interim Assistant Principal
Robert Docs
Karl Olsen, (Jarrett Fankhauser Chair, Endowed by the Paul Ogle Foundation)
Michael Chmilewski

Flute
Kathleen Karr, Principal (Elaine Klein Chair)
Jake Chabot
Jessica Chancey

Piccolo
Jessica Chancey (Alvis R. Hambrick Chair)

Oboe
Alexandr Vvedenskiy, Principal (Betty Arrasmith Chair, Endowed by the Association of the Louisville Orchestra)
Alex Dithomas

English Horn
Jennifer Potochnic (Philip M. Lanier Chair)

Clarinet
Andrea Levine, Principal (Brown-Forman Corp. Chair)
Marilyn Nije (General Dillman Rash Chair)
Ernest Gross

Bass Clarinet
Ernest Gross (Kate H. and Julian P. Van Winkle Chair)

Bassoon
Matthew Karr, Principal (Paul D. McDowell Chair)

Francisco Joubert Bernard

Horn
Jon Gustely, Principal (Edith S. and Barry Bingham Jr. Chair)
Diana Morgen (Gary † and Sue Russell Chair)
Scott Leger, Assistant Principal/Third Horn
Stephen Causey

Trumpet
Noah Dugan, Principal (Leon Rapier Chair, Endowed by the Musicians of the Louisville Orchestra)
Sarah Jessen, Interim
James Recktenwald

Trombone
James Seymour, Principal
Guangwei Fan

Bass Trombone
J. Bryan Heath

Tuba
Andrew Doub, Principal

Timpani
Christopher Choi, Principal (Mr. and Mrs. Warwick Dudley Musson Principal Timpani Chair)

Percussion
John Pedroja, Principal

Harp
Grace Roepke, Principal

Executive
Nathaniel Koch, Chief of Staff
Megan Marsden, Office Administrator and Patron Services Associate
Ava Bradley, Executive Assistant

Operations
Adam Thomas, Director of Operations
Adrienne Hinkebein, Director of Orchestra Personnel
Jake Cunningham, Operations Manager
Kasmira Frazier, Assistant Stage Manager
Trevor Johnson, Production Assistant
Murphy Lamb, Personnel and Operations Assistant
Bill Polk, Stage Manager
Chris Skyles, Librarian

Creators Corps
Jacob Gotlib, Creators Corps Program Manager
Alex Berko, Creator in Residence
Nkeiru Okoye, Creator in Residence
Tanner Porter, Creator in Residence

Development
Jessica Burleson, Assistant Director of Development
Mike Slaton, Major Gifts Officer

Education and Community Partnerships
Sarah Lempke O'Hare, Director of Education and Community Partnerships
Jenny Baughman, Education and School Programs Manager
Allison Cross, Local Community Partnerships Manager

Endowment
Edward W. Schadt, Director of Endowment Giving

Allison Pfeiffer, Endowment Campaign Manager

Finance
Tonya McSorley, Chief Financial Officer
Stacey Brown, Controller
Cheri Reinbold, Staff

In Harmony Commonwealth Tour
Elizabeth Etienne, Kentucky Tour and Community Partnerships Manager
Rone Sparrow, Tour Project Coordinator

Marketing and Communications
Mallory Kramer, Director of Marketing
Serena Haming, Audience Engagement Manager
David Sharpe, Marketing Manager

Membership and Patron Services
Carla Givan Motes, Director of Membership and Patron Services
Shane Wood, Senior Database Administrator

Board of Directors

Board of Directors
Andrew Fleischman* | Chair/President
Ritu Furlan* | Treasurer
Bruce Roth* | Secretary
Maggie Faurest* | Development, Committee Co-Chair
Jordan Harris* | Development, Committee Co-Chair
Mary Ellen Wiederwohl* | Governance, Committee Chair
Carol Hebel* | At Large
Winona Shiprek* | At Large
Lindsay Vallandingham* | At Large

Susan Von Hoven* | At Large
James S. Welch, Jr. * | At Large
Lee Kirkwood* | Immediate-past Chair
Christina Brown
Stachelle Bussey
Rolandas Byrd
Stephen Curry
Susan M. Diamond
Mariah Gratz
Paula Harshaw
Wendy Hyland
Brian Kane
Don Kohler, Jr.
Karen Lawrence
Scott Leger
Carol Barr Matton
Michele Mitchell
Guy Montgomery
Susan Moremen
Jonathan Mueller
Timothy M. Mulloy
Akhil Suresh Nair
Khoa Nguyen
Jeff Roberts
Denise Schiller
Gary Sloboda
Dennis Stilger, Jr.
Matthew Watkins

*Member of the Executive Committee

Key Moment in Louisville Orchestra History

In 2014, the LO welcomed a new music director, Teddy Abrams, who continues to revive and re-engage the Orchestra's commitment to contemporary composers. While aware that performance of familiar and important historic classical works is essential to programming, Teddy has dedicated himself to providing a platform for aspiring composers to launch their art and is examining the role of the orchestra to its community and citizens in the 21st century. He views music as the weft of a community's fabric, as the great equalizer among people, and so considers community-based performances and collaborations as an integral component of an orchestra in our time.

— From the Louisville Orchestra website history page

Chapter 3

In Atlanta, People Are Getting Out of Hand

I have a dream that one day on the red hills of Georgia, the sons of former slaves and the sons of former slave owners will be able to sit together at the table of brotherhood.

— Dr. Martin Luther King, Jr.

As a baseball fan, I cared about where the ballpark used to be.

Not Truist Park, where the Atlanta Braves play now, which is miles away from the real Atlanta, settled nicely in a White suburb. Or Fulton County Stadium, where Hank Aaron hit all those home runs, including that dinger off Al Downing of the Dodgers that broke Babe Ruth's unbreakable record. *The Atlanta Constitution*, giving a world-class downplaying of the death threats to Aaron and his family, vicious hate mail, and the loud, racist unrest over the breaking of a hallowed record set by a White, larger-than-life hero/drunk, wrote, "Undaunted by the swirl of controversy surrounding his quest for baseball immortality, Hank Aaron became the game's all-time home run king Monday night when he smashed his 715th."

Or Turner Field, named after the mega-media-mogul and former Mr. Jane Fonda. That was a stadium that had evolved from the stadium built for the Olympics and, while not an attractive stadium, had a positive reputation for field drainage! (Hey, everything is famous for something.)

No, the field I wanted to know about was the Ponce de Leon (pronounced in Atlanta as "PONSS də LEE-on") Ballpark, where the Atlanta Crackers played until, like many things in Atlanta's storied history, the place burned to the ground. The word "cracker," for those who don't know, is a derogatory name for poor, White southerners or, more broadly, any White racist, regardless of their socioeconomic level. No one alive today knows for sure why this team was called the Crackers. It might have been as innocent a decision as the name being a derivative of the Atlanta team from the nineteenth century, called the Firecrackers. Or, and this is just conjecture, it might have started that way, but the stronger, likelier definition prevailed.

Okay, let's face it, you and I both know why they were the Crackers. The amazing thing was that the Negro League team in Atlanta was called the Black Crackers, which might be the best, subtlest revenge payback of all, intentional or not.

Greater Atlanta is a large metropolitan statistical area (MSA) with a diverse population that demographically matches the future of the United States. Of the 6.2 million people who live in the MSA (in an area far larger than the city itself — roughly 8,700 square miles of land, the size of New Jersey), there is a substantial White plurality, but not a majority. If you look just at Atlanta's city limits, there is a substantial Black plurality, but not a majority. That difference should tell you who chooses to live in the city and who fled to the suburbs and exurbs, which is not unusual.

Which means, of course, that there is tension, especially in the ravaging stampede to a binary society in America. The binary-first sprint, a made movement to define what is fair (and, therefore, what is unfair), has successfully waylaid some of the most progressive movements in the country. As we've always known and been told, life isn't always fair. But that seems irrelevant to those who want to drag their feet, both in society and in the arts.

The nonprofit arts sector is unfair to their communities for the most part. It is no different in Atlanta. While artists work to tell important stories (in whatever form that art takes, visual or performance or both), arts organizations continue to reach for the elitists to pay for the privilege. And by "privilege," I mean all senses of the word.

Here, for example, is the mission of 7 Stages, with a reputation as one of the more progressive theater companies in the country. As an audience member and artist, I am thrilled by the art that the company produces, year after year. I'm glad I live in a world where 7 Stages utilizes the skills of artists from all over the world.

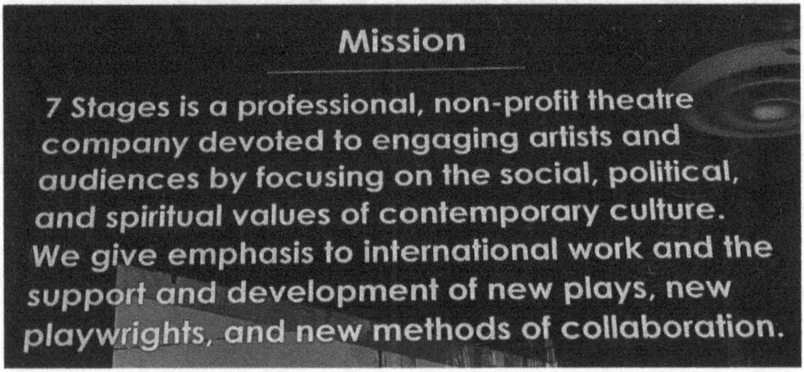

The good news is that the mission is printed on the window in front of the theater. Large type, sans serif, and sets a clear expectation of the art they choose to produce. To be honest, there are too many nonprofit arts organizations that have no idea what their mission statement says, or worse, they created it in an afternoon for a grant application.

The bad news is that this mission is not a suitable mission for a nonprofit arts organization. They talk about engagement and they talk about values. They talk about international work and new plays.

What they never talk about is why. And, of course, none of what they talk about is considered a tax-exempt activity according to section 501(C)(3) of the IRS tax code, as we discussed in the first chapter.

Don't get me wrong. 7 Stages is by no means a bad company. It's a terrific asset to the city. The issue is that the company is just not proving its worth by exhibiting metrics, statistics, or other tangible, quantifiable data that shows that it's helping its community. It tries to prove worth by showing what they do, but not why they do it. Once they do that (and live by the metrics that involves), they'll be fine, and won't be at the mercy of the privileged class for support.

There is one nonprofit arts organization in the area, however, that seeks to identify privilege in all its forms, rather than to pretend it doesn't exist (or worse, promote it). They seek out the difficult conversations that begin the process of understanding. They take the next, obvious step — a step that has rarely even been attempted — and turn those conversations into an Impact^2 (the impact of their impact). That Impact^2 might evolve into actionable, measurable opportunities for the underserved, unserved, or classically disadvantaged (those for whom the halting, energy-sapping progress could be described as walking in high heels through raw meat) while still recognizing that racism is not a problem that can be solved but can be mitigated by the calm exposure of its harm.

Welcome to **Out of Hand Theater**.

Choosing to Make Things Better

Thomas Brazzle, Ariel Fristoe, and Adria Kitchens, center, of Out of Hand Theater

Here are some real quotes from real board members as they announce new leadership for their respective, real nonprofit arts organizations. All of these quotes are from 2023 or 2024 and the organizations, at least of this writing, still exist. The leaders' names have been changed to letters of the alphabet, for privacy reasons.

1. "It has been clear to me for many years that ABC has the skills, the passion, the creativity, and the grit necessary to take on leadership at the highest level."
2. "With an impressive background and a deep passion for the mission, DEF brings a fresh vision for the future."
3. "On behalf of the Board of Trustees, I am delighted to announce GHI's appointment. GHI embodies the energy, hope, and joy of our mission."

Yawn.

For the purposes of fairness, let's look at the active parts of the mission statements of these three organizations.

1. "[First Company] produces great theater, entertains and educates."
2. "[Second Company] creates extraordinary theater experiences that educate, challenge, and inspire."
3. "[Third Company] refreshes the individual, fosters civil discourse, and creates community."

Pardon me. I was mistaken. *This* part is the yawn part. The first set of quotes is the natural reaction from the leaders of a nonprofit arts board of directors to the lackluster — no, ridiculously stupid — mission statements of a charitable organization.

Artistry. Excellence. Passion. Grit.

For nonprofit arts organizations, you'd better have those things already. But as proof of community service? Or as a reason to hire? Mere floccinaucinihilipilification.

And then there's Out of Hand Theater.

How's this for a mission? "Out of Hand works at the intersection of art, social justice, and civic engagement. We help create a more just world."

The work is artistically excellent, but so what? With their tendrils reaching every aspect of Atlanta's famed and dangerous heritage of bringing about change, Out of Hand Theater has become indispensable to the betterment of people by including them in the process at every stage. And why? Because people need help finding the right tools to improve their lives and advocate for justice.

How does Out of Hand measure success?

By bottom line revenues? No, but they happen to be running a stunning surplus, once again.

By butts-in-seats? No, because events occur in various living rooms, church basements, classrooms, schools, and any place where people can convene and talk about the plan for change. There might be ten people or a hundred. It could be in-person or virtual. The message is not the medium. The message is a toolkit.

By positive economic impact for the city? No, they'll leave that to theme parks, baseball stadiums, and all the thousands of restaurants to provide ancillary revenues. Those businesses are far more efficient an economic machine than arts organizations, no matter what the squishy research may say.

They measure it, literally, by the last part of that mission: "We create a more just world." And if you ask them, they'll show you the data. They'll show you stats of improved education from the Creative Kids program or of the social justice steps taken by participants taking part in Equitable Dinners and Shows in Homes. They'll show you who came, the actions they took after coming, and the results of those actions. Year-over-year, program by program, or whole organizational data ... your choice.

The success of Out of Hand is not born from telling, showing, producing, manipulating, or through grand, applaudable sets, costumes, or lighting. They produce work in the living rooms, church basements, schools — all levels, corporate conference rooms, and community centers all across Georgia.

But it didn't start that way.

The beginnings of the company were not unusual. Like many small companies, they did plays and performance art and sold tickets. They lived hand-to-mouth. When they bombed with a project — not unusual for any arts organization — they nearly closed.

Today, there is a logic equation describing the goals of Out of Hand, as depicted on their website.

Art + Information + Conversation = Social Change

Since 2001, Out of Hand has collaborated with dozens of community partners to produce programs that combine art to open hearts, information to open minds, and conversation to process feelings and thoughts and make a plan for action. Programs include Equitable Dinners, Shows in Homes, Community Collaborations, Creative Kids, and the Institute for Equity Activism. All programs are based on two pillars: racial justice and economic justice. They take place in homes, schools, businesses, houses of worship, public spaces, and on Zoom.

The New York Times showered the company with praise, especially during the pandemic, naming Out of Hand Theater as one of its Best Theater of 2020 award-winners. "[Out of Hand Theater] did what I always hope theater can do: not close wounds but open them, challenge the moral imagination, and model ways toward the future."

And, as of right now, they are running annual surpluses and building a reserve. In fact, as of this writing, they are the second-largest nonprofit theater company in the city.

Today, as pictured, Ariel Fristoe (Artistic Director), Thomas Brazzle (Managing Director), and Adria Kitchens (Director of Equity and Activism) co-lead Out of Hand Theater. Their artistry, excellence, passion, and grit, as described in the companies above, is a given. Everyone on the board has artistry, excellence, passion, and grit. Everyone on staff has artistry, excellence, passion, and grit.

Artistry is just part of the package for an arts organization. Passion is not unusual. Grit is not special, despite some pithy, 2016 best-seller. Energy, hope, and joy are not enough.

Impact is everything.

Impact is everything.

Impact is everything.

That's the mantra of Out of Hand. It's why the Atlanta Business Chronicle bestowed the 2024 Woman of Influence Award to Ariel Fristoe. She, like all those attached to Out of Hand Theater, believes that there is no nonprofit arts industry without charitable impact. Anything else would be phony fluff, not worthy of a 501(C)(3) designation.

And that's where they have it over other companies, not only in Atlanta, but in the United States.

There is no better example of using theater as a tool for community impact than Out of Hand Theater. It is not hyperbolic to believe that in order to follow their own missions and directives, every major foundation in the United States would benefit greatly by cutting million dollar checks to Out of Hand. Why wouldn't anyone with a checkbook *not* want to be involved with a company so devoted to the betterment of the community? Frankly, it's a win-win proposition for the foundation and the communities in America.

For funders, it's certainly better than bailing out failing companies only to watch them fail again in exactly the same manner (the hope of many nonprofit arts organizations and the reality of throwing good money after bad).

To be clear: every major foundation in the United States should be cutting million dollar checks to Out of Hand to increase the foundation's national effectiveness, and to guarantee that no stone will be left unturned to improve the plight of every community.

Creating impact is not an add-on experience for Out of Hand; it's the center of everything they do. That's why they deserve every dollar of the millions they receive — it pays for measured positive impact among the unserved, the underserved, and the socially trounced-upon in Atlanta and beyond. They do true charitable work, while other arts organizations, all with the best intentions, do *à la carte* programs to augment an art-for-art's-sake organizational monstrosity.

Oh, Those Crazy Kids

"Maia Knispel and I went to college together at Emory University here in Atlanta," remembered Ariel Fristoe, the co-founder and co-leader of the company. "We got to do a couple of really incredible shows together in college. Some amazing experiences, including doing Anne Bogart's SITI Company training during the Olympics here [in 1996]."

Like the birth of many nonprofit arts organizations, this was one born from ambitious, gifted young artists, trying on various actor, director, and producer personas both on the stage and off. "After college, just like a year later or something, we re-hooked up when Maia was in *Back to Methuselah*, a 10-hour George Bernard Shaw play [about the history of mankind]."

It should be noted here that Maia Knispel played Eve. It should be noted, and therefore is, because Maia Knispel puckishly insisted. It is because of that quality of impishness, that mischief, that Out of Hand (and many other successful nonprofit arts organizations) keeps from taking itself so seriously. In a nonprofit arts industry where way too many take way too much way too earnestly – to the detriment of the industry – the element of mischief is the one thing that will keep innovation alive. It is doubly important to note that Maia Knispel is not a member of the current version of Out of Hand, but her fingerprints are everywhere. Some great victuals, too (or as some say in the more rural parts of Georgia, "vittles").

"Even then," said Ariel, "we knew that there was something special about including a meal with the experience. It brought out a sense of community, of family, and it helped bring us focus." At that point in time, Adam Fristoe, a well-connected and talented actor, director, and teacher in Atlanta (and Ariel's future husband), became the third member of the founding leadership team. Adam had trained at the prestigious Southern Methodist University (SMU), garnering a bachelor's degree in Directing and Playwriting.

The founders agreed on three guiding principles:

- "Bring people into spaces where plays are not typically staged."
- "Reach people who do not typically see plays."
- "Find innovative ways for performers to interact with audiences and with each other."

Their first slogan was *You can't see this on TV.*

2001 marked the first theatrical event produced by this ragtag company with the moniker "Out of Hand Theater." *The Terrible Parents (Les Parents Terribles)*, is a *tres risqué* 1938 Jean Cocteau tragic farce about a dysfunctional household engulfed in whirlwinds of intrigue, sex, domination, and dangerous liaisons. It was not something one would see on television. If left to the standards and practices folks who limit what we saw on network television, even in 2001, it might have been an unintelligible, five-minute teleplay.

Adam, Ariel, and Maia did not want to create just another theater in Atlanta. "Atlanta didn't need another one," said Ariel. With 133,000 nonprofit arts organizations in the United States in 2024, about 49,000 of which are theater companies, it could easily be stated that America doesn't need another one, either. Given that reality, they decided that their company would neither be traditional nor art-centered, but instead center the community at every turn.

It worked, at least for this group. Just like the SITI Company (which disbanded in 2022), an ensemble-based theater company with a penchant for crossing boundaries and producing often strange and rebellious art, this kind of training and work ethic can work wonders as a part of the overall education of the young actor, especially after leaving the friendly confines of a college theater department where much of this kind of training is *de rigueur*. It rarely works as a professional structure, but it is vital for continuing education.

It rarely works because of what I call the "Ren Faire vs Basement" theory in devising a system to coalesce a group of people for the purpose of creating an artistic work. The theory goes that "Ren Faire" art (art presented at a Renaissance Faire, Fringe Festival, or by buskers, improv groups, and standups) uses approximately the same process during respective creations. The key is: they don't finish. They never really finish the process, even after an opening day or night. They continue to work the piece in front of audience after audience – testing ideas, improvising, and otherwise molding a never-hardening ball of theatrical clay. The writers-performers continually listen just as much as they sing, dance, tell stories, or otherwise perform. The crowd dictates the changes — sometimes not just one crowd, but many crowds over periods of time.

In that sense, this kind of art is not unlike the beach. The waves continually hit the shore, sometimes with brute strength. The change is continuous, as is the placement, size, and relative erosion and repacking of the grains of sand. It's different every time we go, although the general structure remains the same.

The other kind of art, Basement, is constructed out of sight of anyone until an arbiter decides that it is ready for an audience to experience. Strict rules dictate the presentation of this kind of art. Because it never is exposed to anyone but that arbiter (the director or the ensemble, for example), there is but one manner in which any audience will see it, whether it is on night 1 or night 101.

Personally, I prefer (if forced to choose) the Ren Faire style. While never perfect, the goal is to establish a working relationship with all the people in the space — including the audience. Far too often, Basement art can be precious and exclusive. When it works, it can be phenomenal, but still presented like a jewel on a pillow. For me, it's the difference between refined individual execution and rough-and-ready group aspiration. In the former, there is no need to participate, only watch and listen. In the latter, there becomes a rooting interest in the outcome.

But — and I know that you don't usually see this sentence often in a book — I was wrong. To the delight of many people in Atlanta, the Ren Faire vs Basement theory is not, in fact, a binary choice. Out of Hand has proven that.

They found a way to start as a Basement theater company, but morphed that polished idea into a strict Ren Faire execution. The audience participation element was crucial, not only to its brand, but to its purpose. At all times, even at the beginning, the community within the venue (wherever and whatever that venue was) was of paramount importance. That progression led to improved performances by all in some of the most unexpected theatrical events in Atlanta in the early 2000s.

Praise for

Out Of Hand Theater

Metro Atlanta

"Brace yourself to catch a bona fide buzz from Meds, Out Of Hand Theater's **wildly experimental and highly infectious** satirical review about health care and the pharmaceutical industry."
-The Sunday Paper, Nov. 2007

"Playful, politically conscious guerilla theater"
-Creative Loafing, Nov. 2007

"**Irresistible**...a highly imaginative treat!"
-The Sunday Paper, Apr. 2006

"Like a sharp slap in the face, "Miss Julie" will **take your breath away**."
-AJC, May 2005

"Help! captures the details of self-help presentations with **hilarious** accuracy... Think of Help! as the equivalent of kindergarten fun and games designed for grown-ups."
-Creative Loafing, Jun. 2004

"Out of Hand is **one of Atlanta's cooler theater companies**. It takes chances. It breaks rules. It chases adventure."
-AJC, Oct. 2003

"Outrageous, cutting edge"
-Piedmont Review, Mar. 2003

Atlanta's "Best Theatrical Mad Scientists"
-Creative Loafing Best of Atlanta 2003

"**The future of Atlanta theater** begins here."
-AJC, Nov. 2002

"Just when you thought live performance had nothing to say to **the generation that grew up with MTV, the Internet and cellphones**, along comes Out of Hand Theater's '30 Below.'"
-AJC, Nov. 2002

"Out Of Hand, **Out Of This World!**"
-AJC, Sep. 2001 Out Of Hand Theater

National

"Out Of Hand Theater succeeds in their desire to create an **original theatrical experience** to reach a **new generation of theatre goers**."
-TheatreForum, Jun. 2007

"Everyone knows that theaters hunt for young auds—those mystical ticket buyers under 30—like the Holy Grail. But for a handful of houses... the search never started. Groups like Atlanta's Out of Hand, Berkeley, Calif.'s Impact Theater and Phoenix's Stray Cat have always focused their missions on young people. All three draw the bulk of their crowds—**70% or higher—from the under-30 set**."
-Variety Magazine, Sept. 2006

"Smart, offbeat, in-your-face Out of Hand Theater is **one of the only truly actor-driven companies in greater Atlanta**, stressing physicality, ensemble work, and audience involvement."
-Back Stage, Apr. 2006

"Out of Hand Theater, an Atlanta troupe, takes on the FringeNYC festival and infuses the usual stoic NYC crowd with heart and humor; a true commitment to their material, and honest direct eye contact make this interactive show **a treat to see**."
-nytheatre.com, Aug. 2005

"Hip, Hot and on the Verge... [one of] a dozen **young American companies you need to know**."
-American Theatre Magazine, Dec. 2004

"While it may have its origins in improvisation, the performance is intensely detailed, disciplined and **each tiny moment is crafted with precision**."
-Theater Journal, Oct. 2003

OUT OF HAND THEATER
you can't see this on tv
outofhandtheater.com

Out of Hand's work was artistically complex in nature, but always accessible. On that point, the company made sure it never spoke down to its participants but spoke with them as peers. As much as they were performing difficult works that were fun for the performers to bite into, they were even more excited about audience involvement. The work straddled the line between theater and performance art, utilizing some of the most interesting aspects of both. "It was all about making the audience part of the event," said Ariel.

For example, there was a play called *Help* (not the movie with The Beatles).

Maia, Ariel, and Adam went on a retreat to come up with ideas that fit the criteria that made an Out of Hand show work, at least at that time. Artistically, their primary goal had been working to find ways to ensure the audience had a stake in the show.

Adam Fristoe

"We were looking for an idea for a small ensemble, something that could be done with a suitcase," said Adam. "I remember, we were hiking somewhere in the Blue Ridge Mountains, talking about it. I have a very close friend from college who loved all the big gurus. Particularly Tony Robbins. It sort of inundated me with that and with EST [the infamous Erhard Seminar Training]. Human response to that kind of input was pretty interesting to me. I thought there might be some really interesting fodder in that material. We talked about the idea of creating an actual seminar.

"You know," he continued, "all of that stuff works. It works by changing the way people feel in the moment. So I think that there's something incredibly theatrical about it."

Help was an interactive spoof self-help seminar written by the ensemble along with Steve Yockey. The performers played the parts of four life coaches. The four life coaches loosely represented a living Myers-Briggs test result. Each audience member (including several shills) took a written test before the play. After that, they had to declare a problem and wear a color-coded name tag that stated the problem. Then they were grouped with other audience members with the same problem. The self-help/cult leader, a Jim Jones/Tony Robbins/Werner Erhard charismatic guru, was played by Adam. This was not long after the suicidal massacre in Jonestown, Guyana.

"At the end of the show, we served Kool-Aid to everyone and we asked them to ritually drink it," remembered an astonished Ariel. "Kool-Aid. They never refused. They all drank it every night. It was amazing."

Help was only one of several site-shifting ideas to include audiences as part of the plot. Lots of different situations that already included audiences as part of their plan. But, even with audience participation and a hip vibe, every arts company goes through a moment of panic – when that one choice of subject just doesn't work out, leaving the company almost penniless.

"*Stadium 360,* a show about football, 2009," recalled Ariel, with a little wince. "It made sense to do it, because such a big part of our mission in the early years was to produce theater as an event that the audience engaged [with] in the way they would engage in a wedding, a pop concert, or a sports event. We'd already successfully done large-scale ensemble spectacle theater, including a wedding and a pop concert, Charles Mee's *Big Love,* and our original play, *30 Below,* so a football show seemed like a good idea."

It didn't pan out. In fact, it cost them almost everything, leading to a near-extinction point. All because of one production.

"No matter how fun it is to make the kind of art that you really want to make," said Ariel, "even if you get critical acclaim, and even if some audiences come in and really love it, it is, in some ways, really unfulfilling. You work so hard and you still lose so much money. What do you have left?"

The Old Fourth Ward

In 2009, Ariel and Adam Fristoe moved to the historic Old Fourth Ward of Atlanta. Two years later, they had a kid named Tweed. It's a neighborhood with a historic feel throughout. Murals depicting Dr. Martin Luther King, Jr. are seemingly everywhere, and his birthplace is just a couple of blocks away, as is The King Center for Nonviolent Social Change, known familiarly as The King Center. Near those landmarks stands Dr. King's famous Ebenezer Baptist Church.

If you walk in the other direction for 20 minutes, you'll find yourself at The Carter Center. This is President Jimmy Carter's legacy to the people of the world, a nongovernmental organization which has helped to improve life for people in more than 80 countries by resolving conflicts, advancing democracy and human rights, preventing diseases, and improving mental healthcare.

"I was raised by hippies," said Ariel. "Hippies who believed in social justice. My parents took me to marches and rallies when I was little, and tried to instill social justice values in me. Then, Adam and I got this opportunity to build our house on an empty lot in the MLK Historic District [the center of the Fourth Ward]. That experience was a huge game changer for me, because we wondered, 'What does it mean to be White people moving into a historically Black neighborhood?'"

Not just *any* Black neighborhood — *Dr. King's* Black neighborhood. The answer, to them, was to incorporate the skills of the Out of Hand experience and grow trust through conversation and action.

"We went hyper local and did a project called *I Am Old Fourth Ward* at the community center, a few blocks away," recounted Ariel. "The project consisted of three different dinners. We invited neighbors to come to a meal. We told them that we wanted to host them and just get to know them. But truly, we wanted to ask 'What's important to you about this neighborhood?' Then we used that to help make decisions about future programming."

Ariel recounted the feeling of forgotten families prevalent in that neighborhood.

"In our neighborhood we've got a school a couple blocks away, Hope Hill Elementary School. Of all of these experiences, that to me was the biggest eye opener. So I, as someone who grew up on welfare — with food stamps, subsidized housing, coops, and even a commune — had never spent any significant time inside what most Atlanta public schools actually look like. Most Atlanta public schools are almost all Black, and most of the students who attend them live below the poverty line. I found out that Black poverty looks a lot different than White poverty. These families, teachers, and students were doing miracles with almost no resources. The copiers literally did not have paper in them. Every teacher would buy a ream of paper and keep it in her classroom. Then, when she had to make a worksheet, she would take her little stack of paper to the copier and put it in and then she'd take out whatever was left. They were spending their own money on that and on everything else. I'd never spent any time in a school where every student receives free breakfast and lunch, because there's such a high percentage of kids who qualify for it that the cafeteria just literally doesn't take any money you can pay them. Turns out that I only sort of knew about racism and the terrible injustice that it has caused in this country. It turns out, I really didn't know anything. I only had this idea of it."

Ariel and Adam looked around and discovered that they weren't alone in their ignorance. They reasoned that if they, as educated and sensitive as they were to the plight of those in need, didn't know about the inequities of elementary school education in Black neighborhoods, it was probable that most White people didn't know either.

Their new digs, to Ariel, came with a new set of responsibilities and a new focus for the company as well.

"I asked a few people — the principal of Hope Hill, and a teacher who was a friend of mine, somebody who was attached to the school's Parent Teacher Association, and the city council member for that neighborhood – if there was anything useful I could offer, and I mentioned an after-school theater program. They said yes. That's how Creative Kids [a current major program at Out of Hand Theater] was born in 2015. Now we serve over 250 students with over 350 classes every year at five schools that are a subset of Title 1 schools called Community Eligibility Program schools. These are the schools that are so poor that their cafeterias don't take money."

Out of the Ashes

Meanwhile, after the near closing of Out of Hand caused by *Stadium 360*, along came a lifeline from an unlikely source: science departments at Emory. "University scientists started approaching us and saying, 'Hey, there's this issue going on right now and the National Science Foundation and the other big funders are making it a condition that we have to be able to communicate our research to non-science audiences. Nobody has trained us how to do that. We don't know how to do it. We're scared of it. Could you do it for us? What if we pay you?' And we gave them a resounding yes."

This is a tangible way in which theater can be useful, have funding, and have an impact.

Theater Emory, the resident production company at Emory University, had become involved with Emory's science department at a special conference. The conference's theme was about evolution.

"The conference was specifically asking the question, 'Why do so many people not believe in evolution? What is wrong with our storytelling?'" said Adam. "We paired up with Frans de Waal."

Frans de Waal, who pioneered studies of animal cognition while also writing best-selling books that helped popularize the field around the globe, authored a groundbreaking book about primatology called *Chimpanzee Politics: Power and Sex Among the Apes*.

"It reads like a Shakespearean tragedy," said Adam. "de Waal witnessed an ape social construct where there was a king, who he deemed as a 'loser supporter' to describe his style of leadership. A 'loser supporter' tends to prop up the people who were the most oppressed in order to hold power. There was another old ape who was angry about not having power. He recruited a younger, larger male to try to take over. They overthrew the king, but it didn't work out because this young ape was no good at ruling. He tried to use brute force as a motivator. It didn't work out, and he lost his position. The first ape regained power. But then some years pass, and the young ape's ready to try again. He and the old guy trap the 'loser supporter' King in a cage at night. One of them held him down while the other mutilated his body. Political murder. Shakespeare, right?"

Out of Hand translated this story into a grand-scale theatrical spectacle, worthy of the Shakespearean-style storyline. First, they decided that the human equivalent of chimpanzees in captivity were the idle rich, because they have food, they have safety, and all they seemed to want was sex and power. The play was nearly silent, based on both animal and human behavior.

That opened the doors for a wild adventure for everyone.

"Frans de Waal's original study took place at a zoo in Holland," said Adam. "I decided to see if I could find somebody that wanted to bring the show to Holland. I connected with these spectacle-makers who I'd admired from afar for a very long time called The Lunatics. They flew out and saw the show. Next thing I knew, I ended up flying to Terschelling, an island in the North Sea, where they have this most amazing summer theater festival. It's called the Oerol Festival."

The company received funding ("somewhere around €500,000") and did the show in a three-month tour across Europe. They worked together with The Lunatics and created a version of the show that had a 30-foot tree made out of steel and a moat that separated the performers from the audience that had 10,000 liters of water. The moat would be set afire during the show.

"We played at festivals all across Europe," remembered Adam. "We even played at the zoo where the original story took place."

While the Emory Science Department plays offered an opportunistic lifeline, it was substantially a different organization once the play subjects were directed from another source. In 2011, the company received a grant from the National Science Foundation – another atypical funding source – to produce something in collaboration with the Center for Chemical Evolution. The play ran for a year.

The work had to be different from the free-wheeling perspectives of the early days of the company. In addition, Maia Knispel moved to the UK to attend graduate school. In 2010, Ariel and Adam got married. Company members started to garner new personal responsibilities that pulled them away from the creative atmosphere – not unusual.

Ariel found the new version of Out of Hand (one that responded to a need) to be equally dynamic to her two loves of theater and community service. She sought even more connection. Creative Kids was one thing. Kids are made better by learning the distinguishing objectives of self-confidence, self-esteem, the ability to speak to a group of people, and the ability to think more diligently about the words one deploys. A program to provide all of that for adults would have been okay, but given her new situation in the Old Fourth Ward, she knew that providing the tools for social justice programs and information struck a nerve in her own region of the world. Plus, as a bonus, she could continue to provide work to artists across Atlanta, especially those in the Black acting community whose roles were traditionally few and far between.

By 2013, she had to make a decision. Adam and she were married and also the co-leaders of a professional theater company no longer in its nascent stage, one that had the opportunity to continue beyond both Fristoes' participation. With the pull of a family and no succession plan — and with any sort of succession plan blurred with the success of the marriage, which would undoubtedly have to bear some strain of working together and living together (something I did as well, unsuccessfully in my case) — Ariel had to figure out quickly who she was, what she wanted, and most importantly, why she wanted it.

"In college, I thought I was on track to be a regional theater director. I thought I would have a life where I would go around the country, live in crappy apartments for a month at a time, and direct whatever someone hired me to direct. What a horrible life. You can't do that and have a family. By 2013, I started thinking about Out of Hand, and for the first time, I wondered whether it was sustainable. I realized that someday, sometime, I would want to walk away and I didn't want that action to signal the end of Out of Hand."

Community service is not designed to help artists. Artists at a nonprofit are designed to serve the community. Frankly, *everyone* at a nonprofit is supposed to serve the community that pays for their activities. That's the order that most funders appreciate. That's how it's supposed to work.

At the same time, Adam, the co-leader of the company, was fading.

"I was very burnt out. I was working in a kind of model where you go from doing very little to doing nothing else. And then recovery from that. I had always imagined that I would probably end up being a teacher and I had been working towards that part of my career forever."

Adam returned to school, and in 2009 (before marrying Ariel and moving into the Fourth Ward), he received an MFA from George Washington University. Adam is a professor of performing arts at Savannah College of Art and Design (SCAD). In addition, he teaches and coaches actors in Atlanta (both in performance and in dialects, where he is considered a go-to among all theater, film, and television producers in the region), and has a life that allows him financial security, the ability to do what he loves, and time to enjoy his family and friends. It's a good life. Adam, Ariel, and Tweed have given so much to so many people in the region, they certainly deserve this good life.

Out of Hand was already at the forefront of a movement to include that community in the work. They had the data that showed not merely who attended, but what they did after attending. They tied real-life neighborhood and societal improvement by measuring the actions, not something passive such as "positive economic impact," a measurement that does not prove worth for any nonprofit arts organization. They expressed the data to funders in a cogent and honest manner, always emphasizing the growth of the community (and not their own artistic growth, which, while impressive, does not always translate into a better community in which to live).

"We were able to attract funding by making art that actually was useful to people — especially to people who needed help. That, in turn, made us an even more attractive organization to which to donate, which, in turn, helped us deepen that support mechanism and either help more people or offer people more help, whichever was most useful to the community."

Is Ariel unhappy that she no longer directs or acts in the plays produced by Out of Hand? If she is, she's hiding it well. My sense is that she genuinely enjoys hiring artists, paying them, and watching them grow as people, learning about the kinds of social justice movements in which they can take part. To the performers at Out of Hand, this is not just a job with a paycheck. It's a job with a paycheck and a ticket to making their community more informed and more just. It's a job with a paycheck and the ability to track the movements they inspire with real data and measured responses to the issues at hand. Besides all that, they have the opportunity to use their best skills (the ones for which they earned degrees and prowess), namely theatrical production and performance skills, to serve people. They still get applause and acclaim; but they also can claim a stake in the erasure of inequities in their own neighborhoods.

The Souls of Strong Houses Are Found in Their Kitchens

"My background's in accounting." Adria Kitchens, Out of Hand's Director of Equity and Activism and one of the three co-leaders of the company, surprised me with that statement. Not because I didn't know about her ability to analyze programs both for their efficacy and their efficiency — it is a specialty — but because she is so close to the art.

Adria Kitchens

Kitchens is a smart, gifted leader with an easy laugh and an unassuming manner — but she is no pushover. She does not believe in doing less than excellent work, but not because she's a perfectionist. It is because her constituents — all of Out of Hand's constituents — deserve nothing less. If my life were in trouble, she would be among the first people I'd call for help or advice, not necessarily because she'd run to my aid, but because she has walked that path and come out as a true success story. To say that she's merely an artist undersells her worth to the company; to say that she's intelligent and intentional underestimates her personal value; and to say that she is quick, willing, and present to listen to and serve people who need her attention almost demeans her significance as a leader.

She is no less than a force.

Of course, it didn't start out that way. I can't imagine a world where she believed she would be co-running a nonprofit theater organization. But she is, and the city is better off for it.

"I have a varied background," Kitchens continued. "When I graduated from college, I went into research. I was in Neuroscience at Emory. I supervised the research lab for ten years. Then I started having children. I got married at 22. I started working for myself from there. I spent a lot of years creating my own businesses. Then I went into real estate and commercial real estate, which is what led me to accounting. But along the way, the whole recession thing happened in 2007 to 2008. I lost everything."

She was fortunate that she had a space to regroup, but it was not ideal. But then again, after losing everything, what is?

"I ended up having to move back in with my parents," she said. "Then I went back to school. I swore to myself that this would never happen again. I got a master's degree in accounting and financial management, and then an MBA."

But when she tried to enter the job market in her home state of Georgia, with master's degrees, experience in leadership, and a tremendous work ethic, she ran into a whitewashed wall.

"I remember my first job. I was this fully brown person who had multiple master's degrees ... who had to intern. My work resume didn't say 'accounting,' except under education." At least that's what they told her.

Still, she found her place at Every Woman Works, a safe, therapeutic, and supportive environment where women who are homeless, recovering from alcohol and drug dependency, in the transition from the penal systems, recovering from domestic violence, and living in poverty have the opportunity to develop solid, transferable work skills, to strengthen their sense of self-confidence, and to obtain financial independence.

"The founder had been this woman who broke all these boundaries in the corporate sector at AT&T. Her belief was that everybody's a leader, even if they were just going to work at Walmart. She would teach them all these things. Not just job skills, but what it really means to be a leader regardless of what your position is."

Kitchens wanted to learn more, beyond the master's degrees.

"I earned my certification in transformational coaching and transformational facilitation with a group out in California. I really loved it."

Out of Hand Theater works with some of the strongest advocates for abolishing inequity that I've experienced in the performing arts. Rather than having them subjugate that impulse for the sake of appearing neutral or avoiding being impolitic (or worse, forcing them to agree to all sides of an issue when one side is clearly right), they provide a runway for these folks to bring those issues to the fore. Kitchens is no different. Her will grew from the worst possible situation. Worse than moving in with her folks.

"I've had a lot of different experiences that have made me who I am. I would say probably the most pivotal one was with my son," she said.

Thus began a story that some would call a horror story, a tragedy, or a redemption story. They'd be right on all three counts.

"In 2010, my son was about 14. He ended up in juvenile court for ten months because he was accused of attacking two young women."

He hadn't. It turns out, they made the story up. But to a judge in Georgia, that didn't matter. As is usually the case with Black men, he was presumed guilty until proven innocent.

"Along the way, our attorney found out that the prosecutor was hiding witness statements that would have exonerated him at the very beginning. But those statements were never shared with our side."

Kitchens was angry. That anger would not free her son.

"This is what I learned about that part. For the first time I realized that it's not about the truth. In this particular court, at least, it was about what you can prove in your case."

Was this a courtroom where the judge assumed that every Black man in her courtroom was obviously guilty?

"She said out loud that she wanted to put him in jail. Even after the girls said that they'd lied."

"Then, *ten months in,* the judge finally dismissed the case. Our attorney told all of us, including that judge, that in his experience, he was shocked that this case went this far. He was a highly successful prosecutor before representing us, so that was surprising. He asked the court what the problem was. The judge ordered my son to be held back for a moment."

This judge, an adult woman with a law degree and experience in handling cases, was made insecure by the show of support for the boy. She, a loathsome tyrant and self-designated jury, prosecutor, and executioner during this case (in my view) felt as though she herself were being bullied by the fact that this Black boy was innocent — a fact that did not jibe with her as someone who has the power to put Black men in jail and did so on a regular basis. To her, it appeared that all Black men and boys were guilty, no matter what.

Unfortunately, as just about all of us with brains, eyes, and ears know, this is not unusual, not just in the South, but in way too many places in the United States.

"She criticized us because my very supportive family was in court, just about every session, about twice a month. She said that because my family was in court, somehow we were trying to be intimidating. I mean, we were just there. We were present. But somehow, our presence made it intimidating for the prosecutor."

Intimidating for the prosecutor? The one who held back key evidence that the girls had lied? *That* prosecutor?

"But then she told him this: she said, 'I really wanted to put you in jail today because I didn't like the way your hair was cut.'"

Kitchens nearly blew her top but kept it together one last time to expedite this charade of a trial and get out of the courtroom with her family intact.

"I just remember being so angry. I was livid, just sitting there thinking, I'm in a courtroom with a judge and a bailiff. He had a gun. I don't want to say the wrong thing. I just want to get us all out of the courtroom."

That miscarriage of justice, that obvious bigotry and inequity — all that turned out to be her single most impactful experience, one that informs everything she does now. Sometimes, these kinds of unjust battles offer a path forward, but only when you're ready for it.

"I remember asking the universe, 'I know that I'm here to make a difference. I don't know what it is. But I'm open to whatever that is.' So, things started opening up. I started working with a team who created these kinds of dinners where you bring people together and have conversations about how to make lives better. Ariel met us at an event. I think she came to a church and did one of these dinners. Then she called us and said, 'Hey, we should do something together.' And we did and here I am."

Equitable Dinners

The experience with Adria Kitchens's son shined a light, albeit a fragile one, on the plight not only of Black people in the penal system in Georgia, but on the notion that innocent people, like her son, were not exempt from being held in captivity.

Imprisonment in either jail or prison is a way of life in Georgia. The state's current incarceration rate is among the highest in the

United States, itself among the highest in the world. In 2021, 1,372 out of every 100,000 people in the state were behind bars of some kind. That rounds off to about one out of every 73 people in the whole state. 61% of the incarcerated population is Black, as opposed to 31% of the total state population.

To make the reality even more stark, there are currently 451,000 Georgia residents who are in the system out of a state population of 10.7 million. That's one out of every 24 people.

Of the 3.4 million Black people living in Georgia, about 275,000 are in the system. That's one out of every 13 people.

Could an arts organization choose to tackle that issue? I know one that fosters equity through data-backed storytelling every day. Ask Adria Kitchens.

"At the end of the trial, I think that was probably the first time I sat there thinking that my brother and my father have had a really different experience in the world. Not that I didn't know it was hard, but that became the rocket fuel for my purpose. I was working with Dr. Dietra Hawkins, who helped to design our Equitable Dinners program. At least 20 years ago in Chicago, she worked on this style of dinner as a part of the Chicago Human Relations Project, which no longer exists."

The purpose of the conversation was to share unexpected data and personal information. That meant that participants would have to cross an uncomfortable line — a line, not so incidentally, that arts organizations ask their own audiences and participants to cross every single day.

"The idea in Chicago was to bring people together who don't actually normally talk. They would bring people from the Northside and the Southside and purposefully bring them together. It was about having dinner with strangers and inviting them into your home. And no, the hosts didn't know who was going to come. They just opened up their home, put up the invitation, and whoever wants to come comes to your home. They did this all over the city."

That's where the connection with Ariel began.

"When Ariel saw that — she participated in one of our dinners — she said 'Oh, this is somewhat similar to what we do because we always use art to bring people together.' And so we created the Decatur Dinners with her."

The Decatur Dinners were the opening salvo of what would later be called the Equitable Dinners program at Out of Hand, something for which they have made great strides in gaining buy-in and commitments from strangers to solve or mitigate specific social problems. The timing of that contact, as it happened, turned out to be one of the most successful in Out of Hand's history.

"My company closed down," said Kitchens. "When they did that, Ariel asked me to come work with Out of Hand. She can be very persuasive, you know."

Here was the premise of Decatur Dinners: it all started when a Decatur, Georgia mother wanted to do something to end the disparities between students of color and their White peers in Decatur City Schools. Students of color were being disproportionately disciplined, faced opportunity gaps White students did not, and were falling behind academically in a community that prides itself on its progressive values.

"I went to a Chicago Dinners," recalled Ariel. "There was no theater or other art. I liked it but getting the conversation started was difficult and awkward. So I contacted One Small Change — the organizers — and got Adria. I asked her to coffee, and to consider collaborating with me. Then I invited One Small Change to the Shows in Homes I was doing then. They came to a performance at a home in Decatur, and we dreamed up Decatur Dinners that night after the show: basically adding theater to Chicago Dinners."

Over nine months, Out of Hand and One Small Change partnered with the City of Decatur's Better Together Board, City of Decatur Schools, and the Decatur Housing Authority to create Decatur Dinners. On August 25 of that year, 1,200 people gathered throughout Decatur to share a meal and have a facilitated conversation about race and equity in their community. The evening was launched by a one-person play commissioned specifically for the event and for highlighting the problem.

After the first Decatur Dinners, there was a waiting list of people who wanted to host and attend. It was a great indicator that this kind of program, this path to full participation would allow an arts organization to use its art as a tool to improve the lives of the people they served (instead of merely entertaining them).

"And that's how Equitable Dinners was born," Kitchens remembered with a big smile.

The Equitable Dinners program, an expansion of the Decatur Dinners night, now has three main areas of focus.

Equitable Dinners Atlanta gathers thousands of people every September for facilitated, small-group conversations about racial equity and other equity topics over a meal in homes, community centers, houses of worship, and online, each launched by a short play. It is a partnership between Out of Hand and the National Center for Civil and Human Rights, the Mayor's Office, The King Center, Fulton County Remembrance Coalition, Partnership for Southern Equity, and Atlanta Public Schools, among others. Equitable Dinners Atlanta marks the anniversary of the Atlanta Race Massacre, addressing the history of racial violence, its legacy on the present, and how to move forward to a better future.

"To spend two hours engaged in a public discussion of what many of us are thinking about all day anyway is to create a momentary equilibrium between ourselves and our world" (Jesse Green, *The New York Times*).

Equitable Dinners at Work combines art, information, and small-group conversation to give employers the tools to work effectively in teams, build meaningful relationships, and navigate a rapidly changing landscape. These Dinners support the needs of businesses by providing meaningful opportunities for empathy and engagement with the experiences of people of diverse identities and backgrounds. In addition, they increase ease in naming and discussing equity, diversity, and inclusion issues in the workplace, as well as giving leaders the tools to manage successful collaborations and more effective communication.

Finally, Thriving Together Atlanta is a Bloomberg Philanthropies Public Art Challenge winner and is a collaboration between the City of Atlanta Mayor's Office of Cultural Affairs, the Centers for Disease Control (CDC) Foundation, the National Black Arts Festival, and Out of Hand. Over the next two years, Thriving Together Atlanta will include Equitable Dinners experiences, a mobile art gallery, murals created by Atlanta artists, and an arts cultural festival, all centered around racial equity and how it impacts health outcomes.

The first Equitable Dinners event I attended was on a Sunday afternoon in the basement of the Virginia-Highland Church. This was a progressive Christian church near the heart of the city. This was the sign out front:

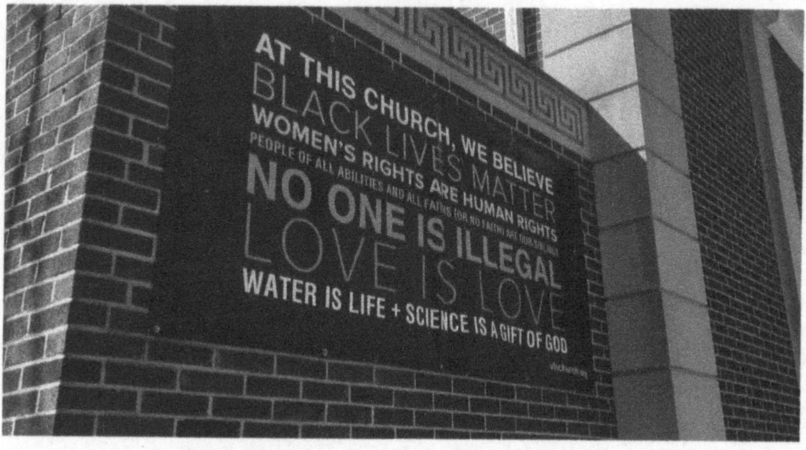

They meant it, too. Everyone was indeed accepting of all faiths, and even this Jewish writer from the far corner of the country was welcomed with open arms.

We sat down to a potluck lunch, complete with sandwiches, potato salad, fruit, and cold (non-alcoholic) drinks. With the brochures on the table talking about the experience – an experience that not only includes the audience but relies on it to change the community for the better – the group was presented the rules of the performance right before it began.

A greeter, the host for the event, asked everyone to pick up a brochure and read along while she repeated the events that would happen that day. The crowd was receptive (many had taken part in an Equitable Dinner before this one, but not nearly all) and had a clear idea what was to come. The crowd was mostly Black people, a dozen or so White people, along with the artists and facilitators. Each table had a facilitator as well as, for the most part, perfect strangers. Out of Hand believes (as do I) that strangers at a table take away any negative baggage from a group and allow them to behave civilly, with a great deal of thought behind their words, and with a great deal of tolerance. At our table, the facilitator was adept at asking the right questions of the group of eight. Great training was evident and it paid off with vibrant discussion, along with a special bonus: commitments.

Here was that brochure, describing the coming events of the day and the rules of engagement. Again, please take note of the partners for Thriving Together Atlanta. These are companies whose purpose is to make Atlanta a more equitable place to live and have shown it through their hard work, ability to collaborate, and a great deal of financial resource management.

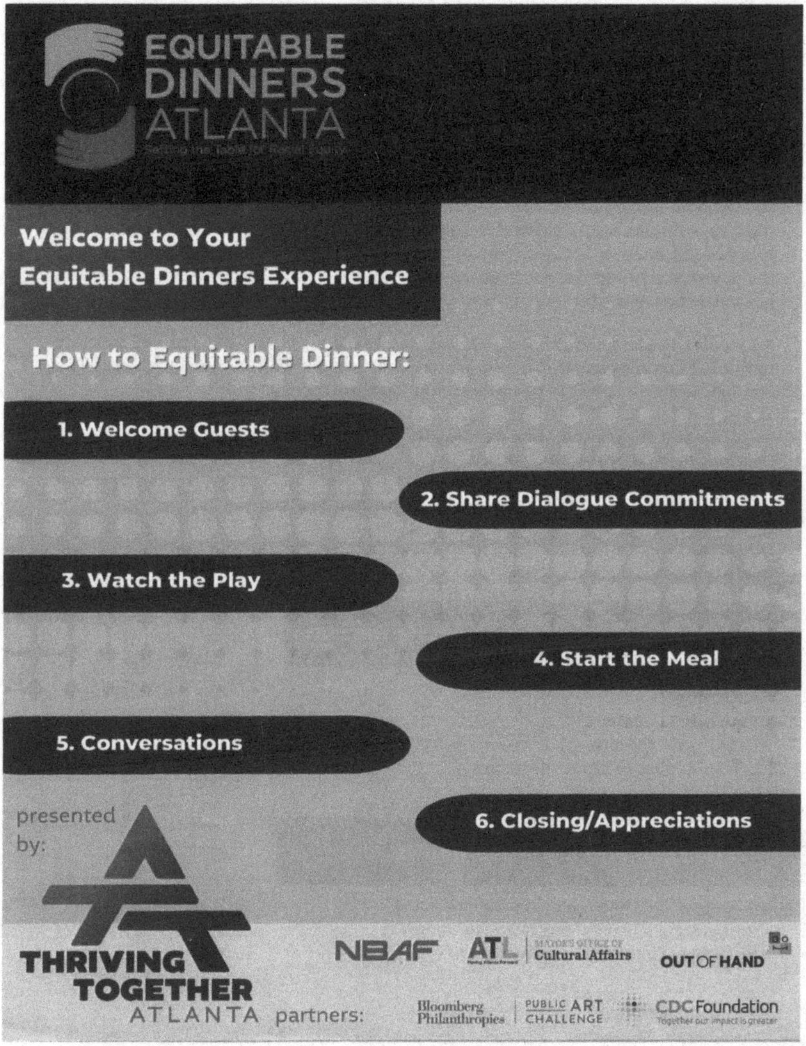
EQUITABLE DINNERS ATLANTA
Welcome to Your Equitable Dinners Experience
How to Equitable Dinner:
1. Welcome Guests
2. Share Dialogue Commitments
3. Watch the Play
4. Start the Meal
5. Conversations
6. Closing/Appreciations
presented by:
THRIVING TOGETHER ATLANTA
NBAF
ATL
Cultural Affairs
OUT OF HAND
partners:
Bloomberg Philanthropies
PUBLIC ART CHALLENGE
CDC Foundation
Together our impact is greater

Welcome:

Hello and welcome to Equitable Dinners presented by Thriving Together Atlanta. I am your host for today's performance. Thriving Together Atlanta is a collaboration between the City of Atlanta Mayor's Office of Cultural Affairs, the CDC Foundation, National Black Arts Festival, and Out of Hand Theater. Our mission is to engage communities through the power of arts and culture, to educate, empower, and mobilize individuals towards positive action and a thriving more equitable Atlanta.

Equitable Dinners brings together strangers and friends from diverse backgrounds to talk about complex issues like race over a meal, fueled by theater. We invite you to connect and be inspired in this transformational experience.

Today we will enjoy a short one-person play. Then each unique table will enjoy a delicious meal, share stories, participate in a guided conversation, and be inspired to make a positive difference. A trained facilitator at every table will help participants engage in dialogue with depth, honesty, and mutual respect.

Please see your Conversation Guide for the amazing partners and sponsors who have made this event possible. Thank you.

Four Key Messages When Naming Racism

- Racism exists
- Racism is a system
- Racism saps the strength of the whole society
- and we can act to dismantle racism

Jones CP. Seven Values Targets for Anti-Racism Action.
Presentation September 21, 2020 to the Duke Global Health Institute, Duke University.

Achieving Health Equity Requires:

- Valuing all individuals and populations equally
- Recognizing and rectifying historical injustices
- Providing resources according to need

Jones CP. Systems of Power, Axes of Inequity: Parallels.
Intersections, Braiding the Strands. Medical Care 2014; 52 (10 Suppl 3):S71-S75

Facilitator Welcome

Instructions: Facilitators please share your name, why you are passionate about facilitating, and three key takeaways:

- **No one here is to blame, we are here to move forward together in a positive direction.**
- **This story represents one person's experience. Please lean into your own experience as a place of connection.**
- **Solutions come with continued and intentional work. Please stay connected to the process**

Courageous Dialogue

Equitable Dinners Commitments for Courageous Dialogue:

Facilitator: Read and ask for participant agreement to commitments.

- **Courageous presence.** We commit to staying in the conversation even when our feelings may seem big and seem uncomfortable. Feel free to take space if you need to gather your thoughts or just need a break.
- **Courageous listening.** We commit to listening to hear what others are saying instead of forming a reply.
- **Courageous inclusivity.** We make room and we make time for everyone's voice at the table.
- **Courageous hope.** We commit to being open to the possibility that things can change.
- **Courageous kindness.** We commit to engage each other with kindness and commit to being considerate even when we disagree.
- **Courageous sharing.** We commit to share honestly from our personal experiences.
- **Courageous care.** We commit to care for each other by holding each other's stories in confidence. We commit to care for ourselves and our own feelings and needs.

Welcome to the conversation. Use these questions as a guide to honest, courageous dialogue.

1. Share your name. Is there a moment in the play that felt particularly relatable to you, and if so, why did it resonate with you?

2: Share about a specific time when you saw a situation get better because things like food, money, or supplies were given to people based on who needed them most? How did it help those people and make things better for everyone?

3: How can understanding the ways racism weakens our communities help us come together to find strengths and solutions that benefit everyone?

4: What is one thing you can do to help our families and communities thrive? What support and resources would you need to make this happen?

Please take our short survey

SCAN ME

THRIVING TOGETHER
ATLANTA
Public Art for Public Health
Featuring: "Conditional Care: Gabe's Story"
Written and Directed by Nikki Young
Nikki Young, a Pittsburgh, PA native, earned a BA from Georgetown University. Through her film company, Nikkiyo Films, she wrote, directed, and produced two short films "WINNING LISA" and "WHISTLE LESSON". She also produced the theatre production Medley of a Playwright: A Tribute to the Life and Work of August Wilson, featuring scenes from the playwright's epic ten-play cycle for the Southwest Arts Center. She was named an August Wilson Center Fellow in 2013. In addition to her work as a freelance writer, director and performer, her production credits include Abduction, Jack Reacher, and the Netflix film adaptation of Ma Rainey's Black Bottom.
Equitable Dinners Community Partners
NATIONAL CENTER FOR CIVIL AND HUMAN RIGHTS
OUT OF HAND
DREW
BothAnd PARTNERS
CLEVELAND DINNERS
Compassionate Atlanta
Racial Healing
EMORY

Conditional Care: Gabe's Story, by Nikki Young, was a one-person, one-act play that took place in an examination room of a primary care physician. The patient, played with a smooth, natural, unapologetic quality by Markell Williams, was talking on his cell phone, telling his cousin on the other end how nervous he was about being there. An invisible nurse thanked him for coming and gave him a slew of new forms to complete — on top of the forms he had already completed. No explanation, of course, but an action that, to the uninitiated, came across as unnecessarily bureaucratic and faceless. It affected this patient, having not been to the doctor for an examination in quite a while, as more than off-putting. It raised his anxiety level.

The doctor (also invisible) arrived to ask him still more questions. The play was not some two-dimensional melodrama. The doctor was not the "bad guy" here, nor was the patient the "good guy." Both were just guys. Guys with issues about the ways, subtle and flagrant, well-intentioned or malicious, that the healthcare system has inflicted inequitable practices on Black people, both men and women.

While I won't give away more details from the play (you should see it yourself, or at least read it), suffice it to say that the general message was that inequity toward Black people is both subtly and obviously pervasive in parts of life I had not even expected. I knew from research with friends that, sadly, just about every Black person is asked whether they have gunshot wounds (something that never happens to White people), but I was unaware as to the extent by which Black people are made to feel uneasy, even in a simple examination. It might be the reason why Black people have a life expectancy of 70.8 years (CDC data from 2023, so the COVID-19 pandemic was included), a full six years less than White people. When you don't trust the medical system to help you (and let's be honest, they've been using Black people as experimental pin cushions for decades, if not centuries), you tend not to get vaccinations, boosters, checkups, and blood tests. Not to mention that fear, anxiety, and poverty are equal villains in the path to a long life.

There are lots of issues at stake here, and that's the point. After the play, we discussed the issues and more examples came out. We didn't merely talk about how bad things were — we were asking questions that might lead to answers, if not at that table, then certainly in future discussions with friends and family. Our facilitator asked us for commitments to making life better. We did so.

It's good to know that every participant potentially has the power to change things for the better. Out of Hand then garnered data from its participants, including the commitments (after following up with each participant to make sure their stated action took place), to show that work is being done to make life better. The nonprofit partners received the message that their work was reaching new people. The problem, a bigger one than can be tackled in one fell swoop, became victim to sunlight — and as Justice Louis Brandeis once said in terms of corruption and evil, "Sunlight is the best disinfectant."

The Disagreement Paradox

If there is one thing that isn't perfect yet in the Equitable Dinners program, it is that the room was filled with allies and no naysayers. If possible, if Out of Hand could somehow encourage those who do not agree with the subject to engage in the process, it would be a more complete experience (a tall order, especially when asking participants to remain civil). That will be nearly impossible to do, but I don't put anything past this group.

Disagreement has — place.

Privately, everyone hoped that people with opposing opinions might have participated, if for no other reason than to use the event to troll those who want to crack the façade of hate. It would enable both sides to listen — really listen — to the fears being indoctrinated on all Americans for the sake of the specious binary battles set up by the media and the rich. Black vs White; gay vs straight; Jew vs Palestinian; etc., instead of replacing the "vs" with "and." The media too often covers the battles for the rich, who munch popcorn in glee as they go to the bank, having successfully divided the poor and the middle class with external issues such as racism, gun control, war, and other (to them) diversions. Then they buy a third yacht, a fourth house, and pick up a fifth twentysomething spouse along the way.

As George Carlin once said, "The upper class keeps all of the money, pays none of the taxes; the middle class pays all of the taxes, does all of the work; the poor are there just to scare the hell out of the middle class."

Therefore, for a real debate to happen and to expose local and American issues for what they are, it would have to include the niggling disagreements such as how close the word "niggling" is to a vulgar one. It's likely that no one believes that they are immoral when they act immorally, or if they do, the transgression is so slight as to be trivial. Or they give the "everyone does it" excuse — or worse, the lame "if I don't do it, someone else will" argument. Or worse yet, the deflective, irrelevant accusation, "well, look at this other horrible thing that *they're* doing." Generally speaking, however, even the most racist leaders among us know that they're wrong. They just don't care as long as they get to wield power.

Still, it is the only key ingredient to full change; otherwise, they "preach to the choir." Not that there is no value to preaching to the choir. Out of Hand improves the quality of data and storytelling in order to increase the urgent nature of the problems at hand. As someone who believes in progressive values and social change, I did not know how much I would learn from the process, and yet, I learned about atrocities I could have never imagined. As part of the Equitable Dinners process, I made commitments right there at the table to write to community leaders in Georgia and in my own state of Washington to get them to commit to change as well. It's not enough, but it's something, and if thousands do it, it becomes a threat to power for those who don't agree.

For those who grew up on *Star Trek*, there is a parallel plot to the disagreement paradox — that fighting one's foe on the turf of a third party often only serves as elitist entertainment for that third party. Even if you are not an avid Trekker, does this drawing remind you of anything?

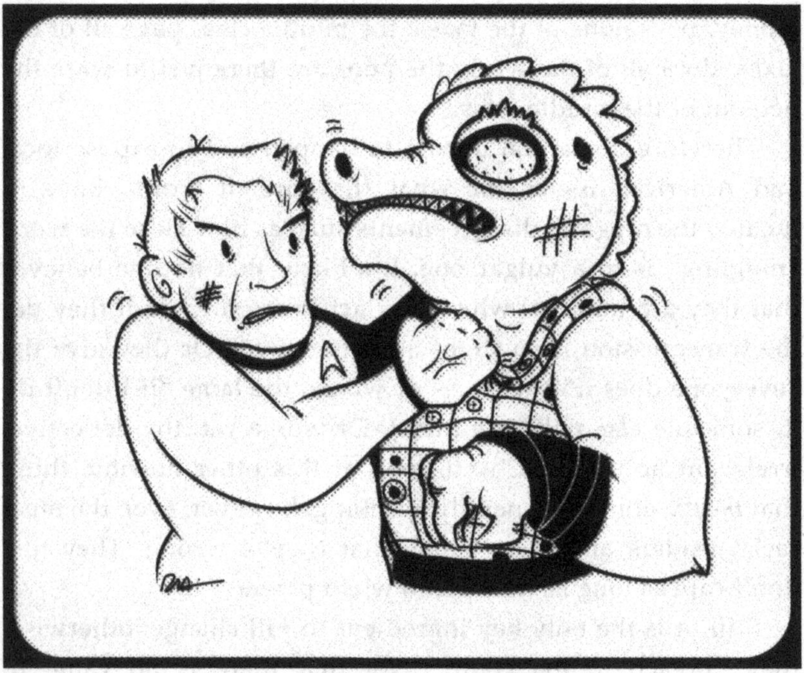

© 2024, Danny Harrison. Used by permission.

No, it's not a still from an actual episode titled "Arena," but I can understand why you'd think so.

In the episode, in order to determine civility, an advanced species pits lesser species against each other. Their stated purpose is to maintain the order of the universe, on their terms.

If we cannot find ways to disagree in a controlled environment, there are those holding those aforementioned marionette strings who would dearly love for us to disagree by force; because, of course, the only ones who win those battles are those who supply the weaponry. That would be the puppeteer class.

Creative Kids

Most nonprofit arts organizations have education programs. Cynically, I know that some were created to attract funding. After all, arts organizations are only charities because someone decided that they were educational organizations. (As discussed earlier, the production of art is not a valid tax-exempt activity by itself.) By introducing an educational aspect to the work – whether that comes in the form of workshops, classes, or study guides for both teachers and students – many nonprofit arts organizations believe that they fulfill their legal responsibilities. More to the point, however, they become eligible for grants, donations, and other kinds of contributed revenue at a much higher success rate when cute little children are appointed as beneficiaries of the programs.

Sadly, few nonprofit arts organizations measure that success. Or provide certificated personnel. Or even provide rubrics that show what and why a student might be expected to incorporate information and skills that give them a leg up on their futures, no matter their pasts.

There are even some nonprofits that reap the benefits of the donations *while charging the students themselves for the privilege of being taught*. Double-dipping isn't at play here, according to those nonprofit arts institutions, because the price of the classes is "subsidized" by those donations. But yes, here in the real world, it's absolutely double-dipping.

In case you're not following the ball here, it means that the only ways in which a student of any age has the chance to take part in those programs — including children's theater programs, which makes it even *more* abominable — is to have lots of ready cash. When the students are offered "scholarships," a completely arbitrary process meant to weed children out (not include children in), they are forced to face the reality that they have to perform, at an extremely young, impressionable, vulnerable age, not only the duties that all the other children are doing, but without the resources for transportation, food, and sometimes, sleeping arrangements. As usual, these organizations force the kids to come to them (instead of the organizations going to where the children are), and if you don't think that inequity is a problem in the cast and crew, you are blind to the usual devils of society that pervade all social situations.

It's akin to a teacher blithely asking each and every child in their public-school class to bring snacks for the whole class.

What if the family can't afford to do that? What if they're living in their car? It's a public school, after all. Anyone is entitled to go, and by law, every child under a certain age must attend school. If you're the teacher and you excuse certain children from bringing the raft of granola cupcakes and orange slices every week, you are telling everyone else in the class that they're either poor or uncivil. You're telling their parents, too. Imagine how many play dates those kids get to have. They become social outcasts, all because you thought it was only fair for each child to be responsible.

Fairness and equity are two different things. If you haven't seen the years-old "baseball fence" illustration that depicts the difference between equality and equity by now, you're just not paying attention. Even so, look it up for yourself. It speaks to the problem of subtle (and not-so-subtle) equity challenges that happen every day in schools, churches, and other public gathering places. Why they need to stop, despite those hellish best intentions.

Nikki Young

The Creative Kids program at Out of Hand speaks directly to fairness and equity. The person in charge of it, Nikki Young (the same Nikki Young who authored the healthcare play done for the Equitable Dinner from the last section), follows the company's mandate to make sure that each child gets to learn vital theatrical skills free of charge in their own school. They're not bussed to some fancy, frighteningly off-putting monument to monument in order to learn self-confidence, self-assurance, and the ability to collaborate. Those buildings certainly exist in Atlanta, but Out of Hand wants no part of that. All that brings baggage that just gets in the way of actual educational and life success for kids who have no financial resources.

"Creative Kids," explained Young, "is where we provide services through the after-school program, or in the school." And before you start believing that this is some frou-frou kiddie theater program, the point is not (necessarily) to train children to be performers. "Even for kids who don't want to grow up and be an actor – or even a director or anything like that – there are so many other skills that theater and acting education provides," said Young.

"Creativity, communication skills, and confidence – all of those skills are important in life. There are studies we've seen that have shown that these kids do better later in utilizing soft skills. It improves their ability to interview and get good jobs, for example.

"I've had parents come up to me and say, 'Look, I don't know what you did. But my daughter wasn't even talking when she came to this class. Now she's putting on plays at home.' I love the fact that we're able to bring that, especially to communities where that's not something that parents can necessarily pay for. To be able to bring it to the schools at no charge for the school. No, it doesn't take away from any other funding that the schools are getting. It's just something that the students receive free of charge with no obligations."

Out of Hand produces its Creative Kids programs only for Title 1 schools (schools that are on academic probation of some kind due to lack of funds, lack of materials, lack of books — but mostly, lack of interest from the school district and the city government). Officially, Title 1, Part A is a federal program that provides financial assistance to local educational agencies and public schools with high numbers or high percentages of children living in low-income households.

Within the universe of Title 1 schools are Community Eligibility Program schools, schools with the highest poverty levels. One of those schools is the Barack and Michelle Obama Academy, known locally as BaMO. Its proximity to the robust Georgia entertainment industry — made most famous by people like Tyler Perry — led Out of Hand to alter its approach. Young jumped at the chance.

Out of Hand provides teachers for 300 students to take theater during their school day as part of Creative Kids. Two hundred students attend BaMO, and the other 100 attend Peace Preparatory Academy.

"BaMO actually has a robust broadcasting program. So we asked why we couldn't do a film program for them. Our teacher went in and we did an abbreviated six-week program. They learned how to interact with a camera, how to slate, and then we asked them to come up with a commercial. They filmed a public service announcement. Then they worked together to make short films. I love being able to go in and see how we can enhance what the school is already doing, rather than having to stick with a one-size-fits-all curriculum that may not apply to the students at each particular school."

Not all companies can be so flexible. Not all companies *want* to be so flexible. When a school asks to deviate from the traditional method of an education program from another organization, rarely (if ever) does the organization have the wherewithal or inclination to create a special program. The reason is that the schools do not live in a bubble; when one school gets a special program, they all ask for one. Most arts organizations care so little about their education programs' effects that they only measure them by attendance and demographics. A few play at measuring efficacy.

If efficacy were the goal for education programs, then the "teaching vs education" issue would not be present. An arts organization — by decree, an educational organization — must prove its worth by transparently revealing statistics and examples of actual education, not the mere presentation of a piece of art or a class about the message of the piece. Certainly, an education program must prove worth by evaluating the future of the students in terms of what previous students have accomplished by virtue of taking part in the program.

To be clear: a traditional nonprofit educational organization (such as a college, university, or nonprofit private elementary or secondary school) does not have the luxury of relying on teaching to be proven effective. It must educate instead. Just as the Louisville Orchestra's education program revolves around results (remember the discussion with Sarah O'Hare: the difference between teaching and educating is the focus of the lesson — "teaching" being an act of declaiming the lesson and "educating" being the act of ensuring the students are learning), so, too, does Out of Hand insist on measuring progress. Just because the programs are free of charge and available exclusively to the poorest students, it doesn't automatically mean that education is happening.

Because of their flexibility and their mission-driven north star, Out of Hand can be flexible enough to tailor the program to the students' needs, whenever possible. They provide the rubrics, work individually with the students (as well as collectively, of course), and fit their work to the school's needs instead of the other way around.

It takes more effort, but that doesn't matter. Teaching is easy. Educating is hard. As President John F. Kennedy once said in a speech at Rice University in Texas, "We choose to go to the moon. We choose to go to the moon in this decade and do the other things, *not because they are easy, but because they are hard,* because that goal will serve to organize and measure the best of our energies and skills, because that challenge is one that we are willing to accept, one we are unwilling to postpone, and one which we intend to win, and the others, too."

Assuming that life happens only once, it is important to use your skills as an educator to educate. Those kids will never have another chance to learn, right then, right there, what a skilled educator can provide them. A skilled educator is not one who knows the curriculum by heart; rather, a skilled educator is one who can lift every child's knowledge and soft skills in order to provide that child a better life than thought possible. At a group of desperately underserved Title 1 schools in the Atlanta region, the Creative Kids program does just that. Out of Hand chooses to do that which is hard – often *because* it is hard – and has blossomed into an extraordinary community organization because of that drive.

Shows in Homes

During the pandemic, the nonprofit arts industry took a cannonball to the gut. The remarkable amount of arbitrary givens within the sector, having grown relatively unchecked by funders and regional leaders, put these pretentious, uncharitable supposed-to-be-charitable companies to shame, and in many cases, to extinction. Extinction is not a bad thing, of course. It's just a thing that happens, sometimes because of nature; sometimes because of lack of nurture.

If it were not for extinction, we'd probably all have been a delightful snack for the nearest Tyrannosaurus Rex, little arms notwithstanding. If not for extinction, Broadway would have to be its own country, because nothing would have ever closed, regardless of whether it sustained an audience. Rather than 41 theaters or so, not counting the XXX peep shows within a few blocks of Times Square, you'd have to have several thousand to house the various musicals, plays, and vaudeville shows that have played on Broadway. Add another several thousand Off-Broadway and probably tens of thousands of Off-Off-Broadway plays over the entirety of time, and you're talking about a lot of activity supporting millions of performers eight times a week.

Few audiences, mind you, but millions of performers.

In response, too many nonprofit arts organizations on the brink of failure (not merely monetary, but mission failure) engage in the crab-bucket effect, or "crab mentality."

As a writer in *Psychology Today* put it, "Crab mentality is a metaphor for the behavior of crabs, which when caught and kept in a bucket, would not allow any of the other crabs to escape. When any tried to escape, the rest pulled it down (shared joy in misery). Similar behavior has been observed in humans."

In the nonprofit arts sector, you betcha they do, *en masse. Sacré bleu. Ils pètent plus haut que ses culs, n'est-ce pas?*

And then, there's Out of Hand. Because their goals and mission are unquestionably charitable, the pandemic hit their work a little differently. They moved their Equitable Dinners into Zoom sessions, for example. But once the heart of the pandemic was over (because it will never be completely over; we'll forever be locked into the Pre-Post-Pandemic Era until it stops debilitating people, and we still don't really know the effects of long-term COVID), they resumed one of their signature programs, Shows In Homes.

They proved, and continue to prove again and again, that the power of the arts and the ownership of a venue are two completely different things. In fact, they've proved that the venue can often be a hindrance, rather than a benefit, to the company's work. From personal experience at ArtsWest in Seattle, where I served as the executive director for six years, I can attest to the fact that fifteen floods in the first six months of my tenure did little to argue that owning a building was a good thing.

Shows in Homes takes place, literally, in the home of a host family. Others become aware of the show through regular advertising and tremendous word-of-mouth led by that host. Unlike Equitable Dinners, Shows in Homes does not necessarily break up into structured discussion groups either before or after the performance. Instead, over some easy hors d'oeuvres and beverages (or whatever the host wants to serve), there is a lot of discussion about what is to come. It is not unlike the kind of discussion that happens in a theater lobby before Act One, but the difference is the shared intimacy of being in someone's home.

Dionna D. Davis (right), the solo performer in "Class Dismissed" by Paris Crayton III, enjoys a bite and an intimate conversation with an audience member.

At the event I attended, in a private home (not a mansion – just a very nice home) in the Grant Park area of Atlanta, Out of Hand presented *Class Dismissed*, a one-person, several character play by Atlanta's Paris Crayton III. While normally, the announcement of production partners usually elicits a yawn from the gathered (yes, curtain speech givers, it does, especially when you drone on about thanking funders), these were not companies usually associated with a play. BLACC (the Black Leadership AIDS Crisis Coalition), the American Civil Liberties Union of Georgia, and the AIDS Healthcare Foundation, through its colossally successful "We the People" marches across the country — these companies led the way for *Class Dismissed* to be seen and heard, close-up, personal, and in the most welcoming way possible.

Class Dismissed concerned several generations of Black women in the Atlanta area. On the surface, it was about Georgia's heinous "Divisive Concept" laws that had been passed in the early 2020s, laws that opened the pathway for fearful Whites to ban teachings that could make White children uncomfortable, even if the books supported the curriculum. Burning books. Teachers fired. Education lost. Black history nullified, once again.

They describe nine separate prohibited race-related ideas, but no further clarification as to what constitutes those ideas. It officially bans the teaching that, "(A) One race or ethnicity is inherently superior to another race or ethnicity; (B) The United States of America and the State of Georgia are fundamentally or systemically racist; (C) An individual, solely because of his or her race, skin color, or ethnicity, is inherently racist or oppressive, whether consciously or subconsciously; (D) An individual should be discriminated against or receive adverse treatment solely or partly because of his or her race, skin color, or ethnicity; (E) An individual's moral character is inherently determined by his or her race, skin color, or ethnicity; (F) An individual, because of his or her race, skin color, or ethnicity, bears responsibility for actions committed by other individuals of the same race, skin color, or ethnicity, whether past or present; (G) An individual should feel discomfort, guilt, anguish, or any other form of psychological distress because of his or her race, skin color, or ethnicity; (H) Meritocracy or traits such as a hard work ethic are racist or were created by individuals of a particular race to oppress individuals of another race; or (I) Any form of race or ethnic scapegoating or race or ethnic stereotyping."

The purpose, one supposes, is that racists don't want to be called racists. That sentence, all by itself, bars this book from being taught in Georgia public schools.

In the play, a teacher is called on the carpet and ultimately fired because she taught from a book that she herself bought at the school's book fair that fall. *Class Dismissed* is based on a true story.

Last year, we went to a Shows in Homes production about Shirley Chisholm. But whether it's talking about banned books, whether it's talking about the first Black woman who ran for president, these performances allow you to explore conflict in a safe environment. You learn how to have these thorny conversations. The only way I feel like we're going to get back to each other as a society, a society that includes disagreements, is to find ways to have difficult conversations in a safe way. That's the only way we're ever going to change hearts and minds. And the fact that we're in a living room — that's about as safe a place as you can get.

— Audience member, Class Dismissed

Class Dismissed is not entirely about the Divisive Concepts laws. It's not about the banned books laws that came after them. That's the platform from which Crayton dives into multi-generational inequity, both for Black people and for women, in Georgia, the Deep South, and the rest of the United States. In it, we hear, and in my case, learn about the harrowing story of Lake Lanier.

Lake Lanier is the reservoir and hydroelectric source for the city of Atlanta and its environs. It is not a natural lake.

As late as the 1950s, the town of Oscarville, a small Black community of about 1,100 people, inhabited the area. The town was infamous for a 1912 lynching of two Black men who were being held (but not convicted — no trial ever occurred) on suspicion of rape and murder of two White women in separate assault cases.

Following the second alleged assault, a sixteen-year-old Black boy, under extreme duress inflicted by White law enforcement, confessed, and implicated accomplices. Rob Edwards was one of the men arrested and held in the small jail. He was taken from the jail by a White mob and shot and beaten to death, and his body was hanged from a telephone pole.

Soon after, a group of men called "The Night Riders," a precursor to the Ku Klux Klan, terrorized all the city's Black citizens, warning them to leave in 24 hours or be killed. Those who resisted were subjected to shots fired into their homes and their livestock killed. An estimated 98% of the Black residents ran in fear with none of their belongings.

The town of Oscarville, complete with its city monuments, buildings, and cemeteries, was destroyed to make way for Lake Lanier. In 1956, Buford Dam was opened to flood the area. Divers with the Army Corps of Engineers reported that they encountered a large number of body parts while underwater. This was a lake built to destroy the memory of the horrible acts of White fascist militia groups against the Black people who settled the area. It was built so that people might forget that White people lynched Black people on that spot.

Things have continued to be macabre around Lake Lanier, about an hour from Atlanta. The lake is popular with (White) boaters, houseboats, jet-skiers, and others, particularly in the summer. Over 10 million people visit the lake annually, including its marinas and the Lake Lanier Islands waterpark.

Black people, generally speaking, won't go near it. Is it any wonder?

All this is incorporated into the plot of *Class Dismissed*, although you'll have to see the play yourself to be able to appreciate its profoundest attributes.

After the play, the ACLU of Georgia led a conversation about the topics covered in the play. Unlike a typical, stilted in-theater talkback discussion after a play (especially after plays which require no talkback discussions), the crowd was immediately involved. Again, it's a living room. Crosstalk was rampant. It was lively, a little chaotic — in essence, a party about something that mattered.

After the semi-structured discussion with the audience, Dionna D. Davis (the actress), Ariel, and the representative from the ACLU, there was the typical unofficial banter among guests as they helped to clean up. Each conversation induced other relevant conversations, which induced offers to help, and by "help," I don't just mean they put the dishes in the sink. Here were some of their comments:

"When the whole George Floyd thing [the murder of George Floyd in Minnesota by a police officer who jammed his knee down on Floyd's neck for eight minutes and forty-six seconds, while Floyd hoarsely whispered, "I can't breathe."] happened, I was working and somebody on my team was a White man in his 30s, who said, 'You know, I know that my family actually has a history of being slave owners. And I do feel like I need to somehow pay for that.' He was all-in for reparations. He just had no idea how to go about doing it."

"We're just humans. We can disagree. But let's look at the fundamental issues without having to jump on one side or the other."

"There's an artist here in Atlanta, raised by his grandmother because his mother was no good. He went to jail for four years for doing drugs, a crime no one would have cared about, but his mother had gotten arrested for something worse and she turned him in to get a lesser sentence. Someone saw his artwork in prison and so he was given a scholarship to an art school. He took that and ran with it, but I'm wondering if any of this would have happened if he wasn't so impaired to achieve because he was poor and Black. Not poor or Black — poor and Black."

Shows in Homes is a throwback to the original purpose of theater: to tell the stories of the day in order to put context into the lives of the people affected by those stories. The plays commissioned by Out of Hand are neither for the critics nor the storyteller. They are for people who want to make a difference. After dozens of performances of Shows in Homes, more people take more action to positively affect the lives of those around them. Because these stories are hyper-local in nature, there are literally hundreds of ideas that, when enacted, help Atlanta become a better place to live.

Thomas Brazzle – Making It Matter

"I think the benefit we have is being mobile. We don't have a brick-and-mortar place that everyone has to find. We apply inside-out thinking in terms of inside the community."

Thomas Brazzle

There are three leaders at Out of Hand Theater. Thomas Brazzle, the managing director, possesses the difficult skill of being able to sharply bring priorities into focus. Not coincidentally, like Ariel Fristoe and Adria Kitchens, he's brilliant. He's also an artist himself, which makes his contributions to the company even more perspective driven.

"Speaking for myself, as an actor, director, and writer, I know when I've done productions, the ones that have meant so much to me – the ones that connected with me – are the ones where I can tell that the organization that produced them did so because of this community, not in spite of it. For example, we've been having a lot of issues with our students dealing with gang violence. So we're looking at the next production from that lens, and we're bringing in people who are experts in that area and can speak to the problem with the kids themselves. So often, arts companies can get so caught up in their production, how to fill the seats, paying to build the sets on time, getting and paying the right actors, and then they forget about why they chose to do it in the first place."

When I spoke with Thomas at length, the company was in the middle of budget meetings for the following fiscal year. While it would be easy to say that his ability to persuade comes from his training as an actor, it wouldn't be fair. Or even accurate. His ability as an actor comes from his ability to persuade, not the other way around. He's just that good at what he does.

Intent and intentionality are his biggest drivers as an arts leader. "I think that artists naturally say to themselves, 'Okay, so if I'm going to go spend my own money to do, say, a mural, I'm probably going to have a good sense of why I'm doing it.' But then I wonder about bigger arts organizations. I wonder about why that goes away. I feel when you're planning out your seasons or you know your staffing, things like that, why does, all of a sudden, the intentionality go out the window?"

Being a Black artist is more than being an artist who happens to be Black. It means enmeshing one's goals as a person and as a community with the kind of art that lifts both, not as victims complaining about justifiable grievances, but as sources of energetic progress and betterment.

"For me, as an artist, it's very important to point out that we're not just living some default story of Black America. Our story is not only about slavery and the trauma of gang violence, the Watts Riots, all that stuff. We had great things that were taken away from us, like Black Wall Street in Tulsa, all these different things. You know, a Black community called Oscarville right here in Georgia was destroyed when they flooded it with Lake Lanier. And there's a resort and waterpark there now, which is ridiculous."

Jordan Peele, that's your next film.

At Out of Hand Theater, they make it a point not to paint pictures of victimization and hopelessness among the Black population. Nor do they believe in White Saviorhood. Like so many collectives of people, Black people are a community that has a history, but in Georgia specifically, what affects the Black community affects everyone's community.

Brazzle thinks about the next steps for Out of Hand and agrees that conversation is not enough, especially with allies.

"My next thing for the company is: what happens *after* the conversation? What can we model as a staff, as an organization about things you can actually do, things we all can actually do, physically in our community? For me, I think that's becoming the next piece of sense of service. We work with the Carter Center. We connect with Habitat for Humanity. Maybe each year, we go out and help build a house. Our only real weaknesses, and there aren't many, are in doing the things that we ask our constituents to do. To frame our plea in a way that works, which is the best way toward real, tangible impact. When we model that, the people learn that lesson. They think, 'Oh, so after I get the information, I'll talk about it. After that, I will do something about it.' And they learn what volunteering looks like."

Thomas has a great deal of talent and connections, and with new and deeper inroads into the burgeoning film and television scene in Atlanta, continues to work as an artist outside of Out of Hand Theater. But his theater origin story tells more about why he and Out of Hand are perfect for each other:

"I performed in my first musical ever when I was in high school. During that time, a young kid that lived on my street was killed when a drunk driver hit him. The young kid's mother was a single mother. And at that time, it was just her and her son. Gone. So the whole neighborhood did whatever they could to help. Her neighborhood friends wanted to get her out of the house, you know? The school was shaken up. Everyone came by with lots of food. The first thing. All the neighbors said to her, 'Right, we gotcha.' And we did.

"As for me, I was doing *Godspell*. And I was playing Jesus. Now this mom was very Christian — Texas, Bible Belt stuff. She came to see the show, first time out of the house in weeks. I'll never forget. All the mothers in the neighborhood got together, got her out the house and said, 'We're going to go see the show.'

And then, at the end of the show, the director had everyone in the cast run out into the audience and dance. That's how the show ended.

"Every night I just kind of sat at the edge of the stage. I was tired. The role of Jesus is in every scene, every song – he is the content. While I sat there, exhausted, she came up to me, bawling. I knew who she was and I'd heard her story. She just came up to me and held my hand. She said, 'I just got to tell you, you gave me the greatest gift. I felt like my son was telling me that it's going to be okay, that I can keep my faith. And I just thank you because I honestly did not have my faith. It was gone. But what happened to my son ... this, this, this. Tonight, I feel safe.'

"My director was standing just a couple of feet away. She walked up and she sat next to me and she told me that it was just the most amazing thing anyone could ever have told you as an artist, that you gave something to somebody. It's a beautiful thing. That's why I want to do this. It's for those people who need an opportunity to be transformed past whatever they're going through. It gives them an answer. It gives you an idea. It brings new life to the world."

It seems so simple sometimes. The art you do for yourself might be fun and get acclaim. But the art you do to transform someone's life, one that is in need, is precious. Helping those who need help is why nonprofit arts organizations exist; they're no different in that respect from any charity that helps those who need help. It is the reason Out of Hand Theater does what it does, and why Thomas Brazzle is perfect for the tasks at hand.

Doesn't your region deserve a nonprofit arts organization that helps those who actually need help, you know, like a ... What's the word? Oh yeah, right.

Charity.

Hahvard, Y'all

In 2024, Harvard Business School created a case study titled *Out of Hand Theater: Monetizing Creativity*. It was created from a B-School mentality, hence the emphasis on "monetizing" instead of "providing impact with," as I might have titled it. Still, it's a document of some note. For those who still look to the dollar as the utmost recognition of success — and hell, that's what they do at Harvard, especially at the Business School — it substantively reveals through observation that doing the right thing is more profitable than doing the most beautiful thing, the most popular thing, or the most requested thing by a company's donors. It places Out of Hand Theater not at the apex of a mountain of activities that can help a community thrive, but at the hub of a tightly spinning wheel of highly sought impact.

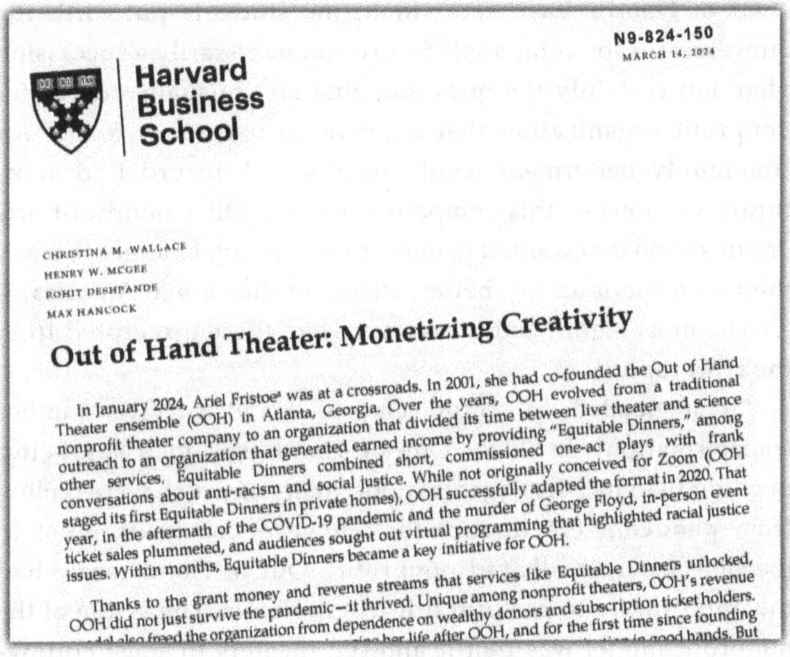

N9-824-150
MARCH 14, 2024

Harvard Business School

CHRISTINA M. WALLACE
HENRY W. MCGEE
ROHIT DESHPANDE
MAX HANCOCK

Out of Hand Theater: Monetizing Creativity

In January 2024, Ariel Fristoe[a] was at a crossroads. In 2001, she had co-founded the Out of Hand Theater ensemble (OOH) in Atlanta, Georgia. Over the years, OOH evolved from a traditional nonprofit theater company to an organization that divided its time between live theater and science outreach to an organization that generated earned income by providing "Equitable Dinners," among other services. Equitable Dinners combined short, commissioned one-act plays with frank conversations about anti-racism and social justice. While not originally conceived for Zoom (OOH staged its first Equitable Dinners in private homes), OOH successfully adapted the format in 2020. That year, in the aftermath of the COVID-19 pandemic and the murder of George Floyd, in-person event ticket sales plummeted, and audiences sought out virtual programming that highlighted racial justice issues. Within months, Equitable Dinners became a key initiative for OOH.

Thanks to the grant money and revenue streams that services like Equitable Dinners unlocked, OOH did not just survive the pandemic—it thrived. Unique among nonprofit theaters, OOH's revenue model also freed the organization from dependence on wealthy donors and subscription ticket holders. [...] her life after OOH, and for the first time since founding [...] in good hands. But

Harvard presents about 500 case studies to its MBA candidates during their terms there. The tasks of the students are fourfold: read and analyze, discuss, engage in class, and reflect on the case as though the student were in a position of leadership in the company being studied. It is a dynamic learning structure, meant to change constantly and offer new perspectives as the students immerse themselves in the data and the personalities of the issues at hand.

As a case study, this one drew no conclusions – it only asked questions based on facts present as an exercise for the students of the school. It neither applauded nor disapproved of the way Out of Hand has functioned, but merely laid out the case for its students to decipher what the best next moves might be. A thorough exercise in educated conjecture.

At the end of the report (available for purchase from the Harvard Business School) came a discussion under the heading "Out of Hand's Last Act?" In it, the students put forth the questions for the company's future; not necessarily a succession plan, but certainly the questions that an unusually successful nonprofit organization that happens to use art as a tool for community betterment would have to ask in order to make future versions of this company (and any other nonprofit arts organization that wanted to make the necessary changes to make their own communities better, wherever they are in America).

The most significant takeaways were these (excerpted from the HBR report):

"If it needed to, could Out of Hand survive another transformation? In 2024, Out of Hand was in a far better position than its peer organizations, many of which were reeling from pandemic-era disruptions. However, since its pivot to [become a services-based nonprofit], Out of Hand rarely had the opportunity to perform full-length shows. The virtue of the nonprofit model was that it allowed theaters to stage cutting-edge challenging performances. Out of Hand discovered a way to create theater without begging for philanthropic support, eliminating the nonprofit model's biggest constraint [that in today's nonprofit arts world, donors donate so that donors may attend — donors and beneficiaries are the same people]. But in the process, had Out of Hand defeated the purpose of nonprofit theater? 'Now,' Ariel admitted, 'we have a board that cares more about social justice than theater.'"

Is caring about social justice more than theater a bad thing, as the Harvard students imply? Of course not. *It's a great thing.*

As you might imagine, the idea that a nonprofit theater company is there just to put on plays is comically outdated. It mentions the pandemic and the years immediately following as being an "inflection point where outdated models must evolve in order for theaters to survive," a quote from the artistic director of the Oregon Shakespeare Festival just four weeks before she resigned. So when a company does evolve, as Out of Hand has done, should that be taken as a threat to the nonprofit theater industry as it actually is? Or is it a threat to the ossified description that HBR gives to this failing industry, an elitist, crony-centered patchwork of snobbish playgrounds still being run for the benefit of White Puritans over the age of 70?

The HBR even described in one sentence that the industry has no real reason to become nonprofit *except* to take donations, which is completely ass-backward to the reality of why companies are allowed to become 501(C)(3) organizations.

"To access philanthropic funding, theaters adopted the nonprofit model, the sole province of universities and social organizations."

Untrue, unless you believe that the ASPCA, the Red Cross, or the NRA are universities or social organizations. Which, of course, they're not.

While there is no mention in the study that none of the aspects of the 501(C)(3) statute are currently being attended to by most nonprofit arts organizations (and it should have), there is no real knowledge of what any nonprofit is intended to do, by statute, by law, or indeed, to whom it reports.

Out of Hand, in its current structure, will never have to worry about the future of the American nonprofit theater model because it *is* the future of the nonprofit theater model.

Let entrepreneurs increase the popularity of the for-profit model when it wants to make money and "stage cutting-edge plays." Get investors instead of donors, pay them back to the extent that profits allow, pay taxes, and market tickets for a second source of revenue. Sell the rights to the motion picture industry, Broadway producers, or other natural sources of revenues. Rather than looking at the nonprofit model and saying to yourself, "hey, we can do whatever we want," know that *the true nonprofit model has rules and responsibilities and thus, is exactly the opposite of that ridiculous notion.*

Your local blood bank can't just do what it wants, can it? No. Further, if your local blood bank is "cutting-edge" rather than immediate and necessary, it wouldn't deserve funding. Why would it ever be acceptable, then, for a nonprofit arts organization to ignore the needs of its own communities for the sake of some play, the title of which becomes forgotten less than a month after seeing it?

At Out of Hand, the play titles are irrelevant. The subjects are important. Happily for Atlanta, it's the stimulation and community action that will always be remembered. The board is right: this *is* a social justice nonprofit, just as much as the Southern Poverty Law Center. Just as much as Everytown for Gun Safety. Just as much as the American Civil Liberties Union, which, while it is a 501 (c) (4) organization, is still a nonprofit, nonpartisan company with a lot of power in the field of social justice.

I suppose I expected more rigorous nonprofit research from the professors at the Harvard Business School who wrote the case study. While they got most of the story of the company right, they never understood the issues that surrounded the nonprofit theater industry in America in the mid-2020s. Because of that, the data skews a lot more toward financial acumen instead of where the company excels more than any theater company. Ariel Fristoe, Thomas Brazzle, and Adria Kitchens manage to make Out of Hand Theater the most impactful theater not only in Atlanta, but in America. If your nonprofit theater company is the most impactful in America, that makes it the best theater in America. There is no other way to put it, except for this small addendum:

Your nonprofit arts organization could be just as impactful in your community.

Just remember that you don't measure impact by butts-in-seats, positive economic influence, or test scores from national data. You measure impact by answering one simple question.

What can my nonprofit theater do today to make my community a measurably, quantifiably, and tangibly better place to live?

Everything else is noise.

Just the Facts: Out of Hand Theater

Mission statement: "Out of Hand works at the intersection of art, social justice, and civic engagement. We help create a more just world through programs that combine theater and film with information and conversation."

Tax Return

For the latest tax return, visit https://apps.irs.gov/app/eos/. Under "Search By," enter "Employer Identification Number (EIN)" and under "Search Term," enter 58-2619780. Or, you can always ask for a copy directly from the company. Please check the laws in your state and the state of Georgia if you have questions.

Staff (as of June 2024)
Thomas Brazzle, Managing Director
Ariel Fristoe, Artistic Director
Adria Kitchens, Director of Equity and Activism

Merian Callaway, Finance Manager
Lola Dominguez, Social Media Manager
Christy Little, Communications Manager
Jaris Owens, Operations Manager
Seth Roseman, Development Associate
Melissa Simmons, Production Manager
Nikki Young, Associate Artistic Director

Associate Artists
Dionna Davis
Amina MacIntyre
Sofia Palmero
Marcie Rendon
Dana Stringer
Markell Williams

Board of Directors

Maya Robinson, President
Jamilah Stephens, Treasurer
Joanne Louis, Vice President
Bonnie Shira Levine, Secretary

Gretchell Aguilar
Paul Barsness
Terrence Burroughs
Imara Canady
Joy Dyess
Scott Gardner
Terra Gay
Letricia Henson
Tamaron Houston
Toi B. James
Chaundra Johnson
Korri Jones
Bonnie Shira Levine
Shane Little
KaeAnne Parris
Cristina Pastore
Karen Paty
Kristen Taylor

Advisory Board

Folashade Alao, Liliana Bakhtiari, Matt Beckett, Kamau Bobb, Merian Callaway, John Childs, Jermal Collins, Amy Corn, Carmen Daniel, Jennifer Denning, Christy Hull Eikhoff, Ryan Esparza, Reade Fahs, Lara Ferreira, Richard Harris, Charlie Henn, Lynda Herrig, Sandy-Asari Hogan, Nicole Horn, Shaina Horrell, Pam Hughes, Kimberly Hutchens, Darryl Johnson, Alex Joseph, Margartia Kompelmakher, David Lynn, Rosemary Magee, Nathalie Mason-Fleury, Atiba Mbiwan, Kerry McArdle,

Nichole Miles-Sullivan, Raphiel Murden, Kerri Golden Oransky, Sarah Parker, Amanda Plumb, Billie Pritchard, Niya Randall, Natosha Reid Rice, Robyn Roberts, Rajni Shankar-Brown, Doug Shipman, Avital Shira, Amy Smith, Kenneth Taylor, Nicole Thompson, Peter Williams

---

About Out of Hand

Art + Information + Conversation = Social Change

Winner of The New York Times Best Theater of 2020 and the Governor's Award for the Arts and Humanities 2021, Out of Hand works at the intersection of art, social justice, and civic engagement.

Out of Hand helps create a more just world through programs that combine theater and film with information and conversation. Since 2001, it has collaborated with dozens of community partners to produce programs that combine art to open hearts, information to open minds, and conversation to process feelings and thoughts and make a plan for action. Programs include Equitable Dinners, Shows in Homes, Community Collaborations, Creative Kids, and the Institute for Equity Activism. All programs are based on two pillars: racial justice, and economic justice. They take place in homes, schools, businesses, houses of worship, public spaces, and on Zoom.

Chapter 4

The Ones Getting It Right from the Start

It was my original idea to feature only organizations that had to make the change that most nonprofit arts organizations are going to have to make in order to succeed. I was particularly interested in those that had come up as traditional companies and had existed that way for a period of time. Then, because of finances or other obstacles, including the pandemic, I wanted to show how they had made the "Scene Change" and served completely at the pleasure of their communities ... and succeeded. The best of the bunch were the Louisville Orchestra and Out of Hand Theater, both of which deserve nothing but respect, rewards, and those seven-figure checks from every major foundation in the United States.

But that approach didn't do it for me. It left out a number of nonprofit arts organizations that evolved quickly into community service organizations, dedicated to making lives better. Just because there was no great moment of change didn't mean that they're already doing the kind of work that charitable arts organizations were created to do.

As a result, this third section is not about a single organization. I have surveyed nonprofit arts organizations all across the country and found many that have achieved greatness by doing the right thing and bringing art to the people instead of forcing people to come to them. One quote from Teddy Abrams of the Louisville Orchestra is now burned into my mind, and I hope it can be burned into yours:

"We come to the people in these communities as their guests, not their hosts."

Good nonprofit arts organizations produce for all the people of their community, not just their current über-wealthy donors and audience members. Exceptional ones produce art *in response* to the community's stated needs and issues. But the best ones — the *great* ones — produce art that mitigates or solves those issues and makes lives better.

Be a great company. Make a positive impact on your community that has nothing to do with the art you produce, even if you believe your art is excellent in quality. Don't skate by on whatever your definition is of "producing excellence." In the long run, it's not only meaningless to your community and forgotten quickly, but it is turning funders against the whole industry. Funders want to fund positive change. The more your organization kowtows to donors who are the beneficiaries of their own donations ("Donors donate so that donors may attend"), the less likely you'll receive funding anywhere else.

Someday, relatively soon, those people will die. Their kids will have no reason to use their inheritances on arts organizations that don't make the impact on society that they want. They have no reason to. They have their own priorities, and right now (as you look into your gray-haired, well-dressed audience), you're not one of them.

Be one of them. It's not as hard as you think it is.

There are four nonprofit arts organizations that understand why they do what they do. They've done it from the beginning. After you read about them, don't sit back and say to yourself, "Well, they're in a different position than we are." Instead, continue to follow them, see where they continue to go right (and where, perhaps in the future, they might go wrong), and learn from them. Remember that they're human beings, too. They could offer any nonprofit arts organization the best lessons in how to make themselves indispensable.

You can do this, too, with your nonprofit arts organization. It starts with intent; you have to "want to."

Voices of Our City Choir — San Diego, California

Voices of Our City Choir (Photo by Amy Huzil)

There is a lazy maxim about unhoused people in San Diego, California. It is the idea that if people were to choose to be homeless, they might as well be homeless in San Diego.

No one chooses to be homeless.

Voices of Our City Choir understands that better than any other nonprofit arts organization in America. They treasure their relationships with the unhoused rather than seeing them as obstacles to community success. The "San Diego" maxim causes more than eye-rolling from this group; it inspires action.

Sadly, there are substantially more harmful pseudo-truths about the unhoused situation in the United States, mostly distributed among those who have never actually spoken to someone in that position. There was that ruthlessly reckless commentator from Fox News, a company that admitted in a 2023 court filing that it endorsed lies to further its agenda, who aired interviews with five unhoused people and concluded, "I think it's clear that homeless people, from the people who have spoken, want to be homeless." There was no data as to how many unhoused people participated nor whether they were paid for their video testimony.

No one *chooses* to be homeless.

The dangerous myth of homelessness being a positive choice stems from a desire to refuse to acknowledge the issues involved. Unhoused individuals remain in the background of even the busiest of cities, haunted by the demons that led to their situation and exacerbated by a privileged class who would prefer they didn't exist at all. That same right-wing pundit once said that the solution was to bulldoze entire neighborhoods and institutionalize people who are unhoused to eliminate what he called "drugged-out zombies chasing barefooted babies through piles of garbage with hypodermic needles and fire everywhere."

No one chooses to be homeless.

The root causes of the housing crisis that has led to rampant homelessness are widely varied, as described by the Coalition for the Homeless:

"The fact is that people become homeless for many reasons, from loss of a job or lowered wages, to a health care crisis, increased rent, a family emergency, or even landlord bullying. Homelessness is driven by systemic factors like the lack of affordable housing and institutional racism, not personal failings. Surveys show that many families seek shelter directly after an eviction or after fleeing domestic violence, and many others seek shelter after residing in doubled-up, overcrowded, or substandard housing. Many families seeking shelter recently suffered job losses or a loss of public benefits."

In January 2024, San Diego's Regional Task Force on Homelessness counted 10,605 homeless residents in San Diego County. Those were just the ones they could find and count; the director of the Task Force indicated that the actual number is likely much higher. In addition, they reported that 22,299 distinct people accessed temporary housing (e.g., shelters).

Unhoused people want to be housed. They want to be seen. They just want to get their footing to find a way to get to tomorrow, the next day, and the day after that, oftentimes in an area of town that might be construed as dangerous, maybe even one that has few that speak the same language as they do. In San Diego especially, they want to be heard.

Welcome to **Voices of Our City Choir**.

(L–R: Steph Johnson and Lindsey Seegers)

"Steph [Johnson, the CEO and creative director], and I hear that San Diego thing all the time," said Lindsey Seegers, Voices of Our City Choir's executive director. "I mean, *all the time* — 'this is a nice place to be homeless.' It's offensive, especially to those who are unhoused. One of our first choir members was a homeowner in Seattle and moved down here. He thought, 'You know what? I'm going to enjoy San Diego for three months. I'm going to hang out my van, live near the beach, then I'll get my place, and then I'll get all settled.' The cost of living and other factors forced him to stay in that van. So here's a professional, an educated homeowner in his late forties, finding himself homeless. When we hear that San Diego must be a nice place to be homeless, we respond directly. 'No, we haven't heard that from the people actually experiencing a housing crisis. Talk to anybody in this choir. That's not what we're hearing.'"

There are others who most people wouldn't expect to have no permanent housing. Seegers spoke about a 78-year-old nurse who never dreamed she would ever become homeless. Medical bills are expensive. She was sleeping in her truck until it was totaled, and then Voices of Our City connected her to housing.

"No one is homeless by choice," lamented Seegers. "During Soul Space, our mental health workshop, we hear firsthand from our choir members about living outdoors, in a shelter, or in their car saying that they want to get into housing. What they're told by the society around them is that they should simply try harder."

Seegers told the story of a thirtysomething veteran who slept under a bush in Balboa Park for over two years. He'd sung in a choir when he was in the military.

"One day, he told us that we'd helped him discern the difference between his wants and his needs. He'd come to believe that his basic needs were selfish wants and our program showed him that it was okay to ask for help because he was worth it. We see people through music and art, having these 'aha moments,' cracking open their own sense of agency through creativity.

That young man, Michael, secured both a job and housing. He credits Voices of Our City Choir with the support, friendships, and motivation to rebuild his own life.

"In our group songwriting workshop, he contributed lyrics that were all about his life," Seegers remembered. "The song was called 'Being You,' and it's about self-acceptance and resilience of life. Now we sing it. We sing it all across San Diego."

At its core, Voice of Our City Choir is not a social service agency, but a nonprofit arts organization.

"Our intention is clear. We're here to use music and art to help people better their own lives, not to do it for them," summarized Seegers. "We struggled about the idea of putting housing into our mission statement, but we kept getting back to what we actually do: using music and arts to help people like launch to that next thing, which often *includes* housing. We amplify their voices because we truly don't know what's best for them. They hold agency over their lives. We're not here to say that everyone needs to get housed. Some may need mental health help. But that's not what we do. We're a choir that leads people to intentionality, to ask questions of themselves, and as they are ready, really open up. The critical lesson for us is that the intent was never to assume that we know what moves someone ahead in their life. We don't presume to tell people what to do to make their lives better. We give them the opportunity to network with their community and find the things they need. We use music and the arts as the tools to help people identify what they want. Some folks like to sum our work up by saying that we give people a voice. We're not saviors. We don't give anybody their voice. They've always had the voice. We just give them the microphone."

That doesn't stop other well-meaning privileged people from expressing their wish to help in the only way they know — to tell Voices of Our City Choir members what they want instead of asking them what they need.

"People have donated used shoes to our members," said Seegers incredulously. "It is true that folks living outdoors are walking ten miles a day from one agency to another and have holes in their shoes. But we had people donate used shoes to us that already have holes in them. It's gross and undignified. People have offered to donate camping backpacks and sleeping bags to our Performance Choir members, which can be really insulting because the majority of our Performance Choir has worked hard to secure housing and has no need for camping supplies. One day, after returning from a gig, one of our members joked that everyone thinks we want toothbrushes. He told us that he's received 20 toothbrushes. 'Why do people keep giving me toothbrushes? Do I have bad breath?'"

In the summer of 2016, San Diego's homeless population was exploding. The removal of 10,000 affordable housing units, to make way for upscale condos and housing left the city's most vulnerable citizens unsheltered.

Steph Johnson — a well-known musician and jazz singer in San Diego — noticed the suffering of her unsheltered neighbors and began to organize outreach that brought food, clothing, blankets, and friendship to people experiencing homelessness.

"There are unique talents in each of us," said Johnson, "and that is especially true for all of the people I have met experiencing homelessness. By providing a safe community space for art and music making, individuality positively thrives. The journey of self-expression is the root of awareness and healing."

Inspiration came from doing outreach and discovering that many people living on the streets were artists and musicians with no outlet. Along with the choir's co-founder, the late Nina Deering, she organized them into a choir and found that their shared love of music offered purpose, hope, and collaborative worth as, together, they navigated their way out of homelessness. They became a musical force.

In 2020, Voices of Our City Choir advanced to the semifinals of the television competition program *America's Got Talent*. You need to watch the performance for their talent and for the special "golden buzzer" moment that only a select few performances receive. The next time you get yourself in front of a computer, visit https://bit.ly/voicesofourcity.

To understand their success as a nonprofit arts organization, all you have to do is witness them. Even while unhoused, they work as a team to make their own lives better through art, which is amazing to behold. It deserves not only amazement and renown, but dignity and respect. They deserve to be paid well for their services: singers and as representatives of the kinds of people their community needs to serve better.

Most organizations that hire Voices of Our City — and many of them are nonprofit organizations unaffiliated with the arts — do so out of love for the choir and its purpose (especially in San Diego). These smart companies on both sides of the commercial/nonprofit line partner with them to further *both companies'* causes. Hiring the choir is an inspired, affordable way to provide support to a community of people within the community, helping unhoused people find their standing in a collective venture. After all, what company wouldn't want to hitch itself to greatness? This kind of collaborative synergy not only shows that the hiring company cares about its community, but also allows for Voices of Our City to press its engagement for all the communities it serves.

Sadly, a few organizations, both wittingly and unwittingly, have exploited the group. They've used the reflected glory of the group's charitable purpose and claimed it as a charitable act. Employing Voices of Our City is a great thing for everyone, and the group is an eager, reliable, valuable partner for any company that does so, but employment by itself (and potentially pinching pennies to do so) does not constitute a charitable act.

It's akin to the deluded notion that producing art is something that arts organizations do to serve artists. In fact, even some duped artists have fallen prey to that tactic, genuflecting to the largest organizations in the hope that someday, they might work there; therefore, to those who have been hornswoggled, the answer to every issue affecting the nonprofit arts is undeserved, unearned funding.

Employing artists serves the arts organization, not the artists. Just like any other industry in a capitalistic system, nonprofit arts organizations negotiate (separately or through union representation) to pay the least amount they can get away with. It is never the employer that seeks ways to increase payments over the poverty line; it is the employee. Employed artists are regarded no differently than any other employee in that manner. That's at the very base of the relationship.

Were a nonprofit arts organization, for example, to make the wise decision to employ Voices of Our City to perform at their annual gala, paid the choir their real worth to prove its community-centric mission (or at the very least, pay the choir's actual costs for the affair), and freely allow Voices to use the host organization's data (guest lists with full contact information, for example) to solicit donations, that would be the start of a charitable action worth support.

However, too many believe that Voices should be paid not with money, but with the promise of "good exposure," especially at fundraising events. It's a typically empty artist promise. The truth is that it costs Voices of Our City a minimum of about $10,000 (in 2024 dollars) to mount a performance, regardless of the length of the event. Because the choir members are people who do not have ready transportation, Voices has to rent buses, pay its musicians, and rehearse, regardless of whether they're asked to perform one song or twenty.

"What's very interesting," Seegers said, "is that our choir is accompanied by professional musicians. All professionals. Generally, musicians play their own gigs until 2:00 a.m., and then come to us at 10:00 a.m. every week for rehearsal. Often at hired performances, the whole choir is asked to hide in the background before and after the performance and not mingle with the audience. While our musicians are certainly accustomed to this kind of effrontery in the commercial industry – 'after your set, go in the back and eat a sandwich' – it's pretty damned offensive when it comes to the choir. We do not tolerate that anymore. While the customers are eating a gourmet meal, our own people shouldn't have to make do with yesterday's breakfast sandwiches and cold coffee and hide."

They may be homeless, but they shouldn't have to work for free.

"So how do we choose to take a gig?" she continued. "I created a rubric of a certain criteria and a scorecard that's mission aligned and also operationally feasible. Is the venue ADA accessible? After all, 70% of our singers are seniors. Many use walkers and wheelchairs. You want us to come at 10:00 p.m.? Our members have told us they're in bed by then. The answer is no. It's less about the money and all about treating people with dignity. That's important internal clarity for us."

It may seem petty to some and silly to others, but providing dignity is much more important for a charity than making a buck.

To those organizations, both commercial and nonprofit, both arts organizations and non-arts corporations, a message: don't just pay $10,000. Pay $20,000 if you have the capacity. Pay more. If you want to show support to finding solutions for the housing crisis, that's what it costs. It's worth it.

Centering dignity. It's at the core of everything Voices of Our City Choir does, whether it's in providing services or in presenting the music. The company is not a group of heroes to be gawked at for their ability to be alive and perform. San Diego already has a pretty good zoo for that.

"It can be exhausting," said Seegers. "Many organizations send people to come out to our rehearsals. They tell us how much they love it and hire us at our price. Others might be moved and all of that, but they still want us to justify the cost. So, I show it to them, as transparently as possible. While it is not our mission to play at other people's galas, we're happy to help when it doesn't hurt our own people, our bottom line, and it gives us another chance to sing. Every once in a while, however, some prospective client from a nonprofit or a commercial company will try to justify paying our fee by asking for special considerations beyond the skills, practice, and taste of the choir. Let alone the fact that the singers suffer from San Diego's collective housing crisis."

If you need to know why this company deserves that seven-figure check (there are a lot of foundations in San Diego County that have the capacity and the stated purpose of wanting to do this kind of work — all eyes are on you), the following is a typical success story for Voices of Our City Choir.

Steph Johnson conducts a performance at their home base, St. Paul's Episcopal Church, San Diego (Photo by Amy Huzil)

In 2022, the National Conflict Resolution Center awarded Voices of Our City the Peacemakers Award. The choir members performed. Donors purchased several tables at the gala for the choir members to be fully included. The caterer put sparkling cider in champagne flutes so that the choir members could enjoy the cocktail hour fully along with the guests. It is a perfect example of how the choir *can* be included in a way that centers their humanity and dignity.

Internally, the members are fully supported. Let's say you were a member of the choir and wanted help in finding some form of housing. Voices of Our City would connect you to one of their social service housing partners. They would even accompany you so that you wouldn't have to face the paperwork jungle alone. The social service agency would give you a number and place you on a list that is subject to the Service Prioritization Decision Assistance Tool (SPDAT). The SPDAT is an assessment tool for front-line workers at agencies that work with homeless clients to prioritize which of those clients should receive assistance first. It's an exhaustive assessment tool that determines need as a competition against other applicants for scant funding.

The SPDAT has become a tool to deny funding, not to enable it. It assesses mental health issues, for example, and takes in other factors such as the applicant's age and whether all one's limbs are in working order, for example. However, simple pain is not considered, even if it's chronic or debilitating. For example, if you simply have a horrifically aching back because you've been sleeping in a deserted vacant lot in Southeast San Diego, you would not be placed high on the priority list of getting housed.

The price for getting housed might be the equivalent of an arm and a leg. Literally.

"One of our choir members," said Seegers, "has been with us for six or so years now. He always says, 'It took losing my leg to get into housing.' He was on all the lists, had completed all the paperwork, but still, he was sleeping outside. One night, he got an infection and had to have his leg amputated from the knee down. He said, 'I was in the hospital, and then I was in housing two days later. It took losing my leg.'"

Because of the competition for the very few available spots, and all the other imposed red tape bureaucracies, housing initially goes to what the system calls the "most vulnerable." Their narrow definition of "most vulnerable" would exclude many of the unhoused people who participate in Voices of Our City Choir. Voices takes care of anyone who is unhoused and between 18 and 75, physically in fair condition, and willing to take part in the group in some way. Most of the folks that are served don't have addictions and aren't battling unseen demons. As mentioned earlier, a large set of them have college degrees, jobs, and missed opportunities. They're simply people who live outside, in their cars, or move from shelter to shelter as the system allows, unable to afford any potential first month's rent in San Diego. Without Voices of Our City Choir (and the funding you provide them), those people would be out of luck. Perhaps forever.

Most people in this country are about two missed paychecks or one medical emergency away from being in that predicament. Just like you.

Just the Facts: Voice of Our City Choir

Mission Statement

"Voices of Our City Choir amplifies the voices of people impacted by homelessness through music and the arts. Members develop renewed hope, personal empowerment, and the life skills to achieve their goals."

Tax Return

For the latest tax return, visit https://apps.irs.gov/app/eos/. Under "Search By," enter "Employer Identification Number (EIN)" and under "Search Term," enter 82-2363154. Or, you can always ask for a copy directly from the company. Please check the laws in your state and the state of California if you have questions.

Staff

Steph Johnson, CEO and Creative Director
Lindsey Seegers, Executive Director
Dennis Crosby, Director of Operations and Programs
Yolanda Sommer, Community Philanthropy Manager
Natalie Bradley, Music Program Manager
Kathie Landis, Office Manager
Enrique Rivera, Member Services Specialist
Naylenie Castillo, Member Services Specialist
Jillian Buretz, Member Services Specialist
Sofia Ziebell, Performances Coordinator

Board of Directors *(as of August 2024)*
Jean Kluver | Chair
Paul Devermann | Vice Chair
Jaci Sander | Treasurer
Frantz Farreau | Secretary

Steph Johnson
Karen Henken
Lorraine Iverson
Jolene Mayer Shumilak

Despondent and weary
I'm low to the ground,
Steps feel heavy, cemented, and bound.
Can anyone hear me?
I need to be found.
The mud of despair is holding me down.
How did I get here?
Where do I go?
There once was a light,
Now I'm not sure.
Am I still dreaming? I want to believe
There's something out there waiting for me.

Catch me, I'm falling upward,
Fallin', fallin',
Catch me, I'm falling upward,
Fallin', fallin'.

Good morning my friend, won't you come inside?
Tell us your story, so glad you've arrived.
Take a deep breath, you've come so far.
It's safe here to show who you truly are.
The music connects us, let our soul be free,
Feel a sense of purpose and some relief.
I see the spark in you that someone saw in me,
With trust we'd love to be your chosen family.

We know your pain,
We've been there before,

We understand,
Hope is waiting and chains are breaking.
Love is the plan.
We know your pain,
We've been there before,
Your light's shining through.
The world's been waiting, anticipating—
Believe us, it's true.

— *Lyrics from "Falling Upward," written by members of Voices of Our City Choir*

Mixed Blood Theatre Company – Minneapolis, Minnesota

The idea of "radical hospitality" is not new. As Sheryl A. Kujawa-Holbrook reported for PBS, it stems from the Christian community, although it bespeaks a greater human community. Those who practice it, "rather than seeking out like members for mutual support, [congregations] seek people who consider themselves beyond the reach of organized religion. 'Radical hospitality' has not only social, but political and economic implications; it is the act of extending community beyond the margins to those unserved by church, synagogue, or mosque. Rather than limiting their public theology to outreach or charity that maintains the unjust distribution of power and resources, congregations formed in radical hospitality exercise a commitment to justice. This model seeks to transform both the believer and society as a whole."

Some of the underpinnings of "radical hospitality" are defined in various sacred texts, as described by Reverend Loren McGrail in 2009:

The Torah: "The strangers who sojourn with you shall be to you as the natives among you, and you shall love them as yourself; for you were strangers in the land of Egypt" (Leviticus 19: 33–34).

The New Testament: "What you do to the least of my brethren you do unto me" (Matthew 25:40).

The Quran: "Serve God ... and do good to ... orphans, those in need, neighbors who are near, neighbors who are strangers, the companion by your side, the wayfarer that you meet, and those who have nothing" (4:36).

The Hindu scripture Taittiriya Upanishad: "The guest is a representative of God."

These are not extremist views. In fact, radical hospitality serves as a North Star to most nonprofit organizations whose purposes are about lifting those who need it.

In the world of nonprofit arts organizations, however, radical hospitality is almost nowhere to be found. Some use the phrase because their leaders (or often, one leader) *may want* to incorporate the most generous assistance possible, above and beyond the norm.

However, when many of these arts organizations come into contact with financial distress, the "luxury" of radical hospitality disappears for the perceived "nitty-gritty" of producing a subjective notion of excellence.

The best nonprofits work the other way around. Community impact is far more important than any structured program.

Yet, there is a theater company sitting right in the heart of America that dedicates every activity, every program, and every human interaction to the notion of radical hospitality.

Welcome to the **Mixed Blood Theatre Company**.

We talked about Mixed Blood in the first book in the series, *Scene Change*. Their dogged insistence on being more impactful than most other nonprofit arts organizations means they deserve a more detailed look.

The core of its mission — "Mixed Blood uses theater to disrupt injustice" — reveals its nature as a social justice organization that happens to use art as a tool, not as a product. This is exactly what all nonprofit arts organizations could do, but refuse due to some preconceived, unbacked notion that the production of art is the service to the community.

"I think it's clear that many of our theaters have distanced themselves from their audience and community," said Mark Valdez, the artistic director for Mixed Blood. "As the field professionalized, that gap grew. Now we look down on community theater, when before most small towns supported one or two theaters and an opera house. Funders pushed the field to structure themselves as corporations, and so regions lost acting companies. Executive directors and managing directors eventually took the reins from artistic directors (who, to be fair, just as often handed those reins over). Our field sold itself out. Separated itself. Now we wonder why nobody cares about our organizations and our work. Duh!"

Mark Valdez

Valdez is no stranger to the field. With a career spanning more than 20 years, he has created a wide range of work and has been recognized with a 2021 Zelda Fichandler Award and an inaugural 2021 California Arts Council Legacy Artist Fellowship.

The company's notion of radical hospitality stems from its founder, Jack Reuler, and its foundation is immutable.

"Radical Hospitality is core to all Mixed Blood does. We model reciprocity, inclusion, and genuine welcoming to build relationships. We seek to make theater beneficial by engaging with individuals and communities for whom theatre and the arts have not been available due to lack of resources, racism, physical accessibility, gender discrimination, or other barriers. We strive to ensure that the nature, content, and practices embedded in our work are founded in integrity and equity, and engage the breadth and depth of our many communities."

What separates Mixed Blood from its competition is simple. The company does not see its impact as being artistically focused. It does no art for the sake of indulgence. It always intends to serve those who need it, at all costs.

"We are first a social justice organization, then a theater," explained Valdez. "We use theater to achieve our social justice aims."

In every activity and every decision, Mixed Blood ensures that its service to the community is nontoxic, intended to serve those in the community.

"Radical hospitality includes no-cost admission," said Valdez. "We rely exclusively on donations. We have wealthy donors, but they support our organization for the benefit of the community, not themselves. In fact, few of those donors participate in our programing."

"As for serving the public need," he continued, "we are increasingly creating work with community members. We want them to have agency in the work. We boost civic imagination, working around pressing civic issues such as affordable housing, health, and climate resilience. Our work aims to provide opportunities for audiences to do something, believing that if they can do one thing, they can do something else. Our work is driven towards taking action."

And there is a public need.

The infamous 2020 murder of George Floyd by a police officer who knelt on his neck for eight minutes and forty-six seconds did not indicate a new type of local police violence, but a continuation and exacerbation of old racial sores that did not heal the wounds predicated by racial covenants (segregationist legal rules inserted into property deeds and titles that made it impossible for land to be owned by non-White people). Those racial covenants forced Black people, for example, to live in only a few pockets of the city of Minneapolis. Even though those covenants were made illegal in 1968 by the Fair Housing Act, their scars resulted in a 2019 study by *24/7 Wall Street* that named the Twin Cities as the fourth worst metropolitan statistical area in the United States for Black citizens.

One neighborhood that allowed Black residency was near the corner of 38th Street and Chicago Avenue, the very corner at which George Floyd was murdered. As Olivia B. Waxman reported in the May 28, 2020, edition of *Time Magazine* (three days after the killing):

(Photo by Lorie Shaull from flickr is licensed under CC BY 2.0.)

"Floyd's death 'falls within a larger pattern' of clashes between police officers and residents in black communities that 'goes way back to the period of Reconstruction, when a lot of police departments were created to surveil black communities and control and corral large black populations,' said Keith A. Mayes, a professor of African American & African Studies at the University of Minnesota, Twin Cities."

There are numerous arts organizations in and around Minneapolis. But as liberal as the state's voting record has been through the years (it was the one state that voted for favorite son Walter Mondale in the presidential election of 1984), the city is split along racial lines. Among the arts organizations, that community bifurcation has led to a history of large, predominately White nonprofit arts organizations (the Guthrie Theatre, for example) that serve their privileged donors and audiences, paying token attention to the people not included, not represented, and not respected.

Mixed Blood has found that to be both hindrance and opportunity. Their strengths are found in performing social justice activities for those historically overwhelmed.

"Since its founding, Mixed Blood has centered those most on the margins," said Valdez. "As a social justice organization, we want to use our work to influence public policies, knowing that much of the discrimination and bias in place is enshrined in our laws. We're focusing on greater affordable housing, equitable healthcare, and climate resilience. BIPOC communities are often hit first and hardest by climate change."

Mixed Blood produces art that serves and is served by members of the disabled community (Photo by Rich Ryan)

It should be self-evident, but it's often a good reminder to nonprofit arts organizational leaders and board members that *work that positively impacts the least privileged among us benefits all of us*. While most arts organizations believe that their collective purpose is to produce artistic excellence – even to the detriment of including its own community's artists (instead hiring those from arts hubs such as Toronto, Chicago, New York, and Los Angeles) – Mixed Blood is a very personal, very local, couldn't-exist-anywhere-else point of Minnesota joy. It's the kind of work that allows a leader like Valdez to look up and visualize instead of down and weep.

"I want to be of use, useful to my community and the greater society," he said. "Similarly, I want our theater to be useful to its community. Can we build civic imagination to see past the dystopian futures pop culture feeds us? Can we co-daydream beautiful futures? Artmaking lets us build consensus, make meaning, foster belonging, build worlds, and rehearse actions. These skills, these actions are vital to the health of our communities. There is no lasting solution to the giant social challenges we are facing that doesn't include the arts. It's our time to take leadership."

(Photo from 2017 production of "Vietgone" by Qui Nguyen)

When financial duress happens, how does the connection to the community continue?

"Community is not a monolith. When faced with financial hardships, we have to look at the various communities we serve. One of those communities is our own staff. We have a responsibility to care for our staff, the people at the organization who are doing the work. Then we ask how this group can serve our other communities? For instance, at the moment [2024], we are currently producing fewer shows in our own facility. We are doing more work outside our building, meeting the community members where they are — not necessarily with fully produced plays, but with mobile, flexible work that feeds the imagination and creates a forum for action and discussion."

The flexibility of the company stems from its interpretation of radical hospitality. When faced with challenges, they seek the ways in which to help those who need it over those who merely want it. And that includes its own staff.

"There is a tension," explained Valdez, "that every employee holds, from entry level to top management: the balance between mission alignment and amount of salary. We try to remain aware of that balance, paying people fair wages and looking for individuals who have common values, whose skills augment others' deficits. It's not a science, rather alchemy. Sometimes you get it wrong and need to course correct. That's usually unpleasant, but necessary. When it works, though, you feel it. You see it in how the team works. Individual leadership and care for the community (our own community)."

Mixed Blood's "Northside Vibe," a cultural and storytelling series (Photo by Rich Ryan)

Why does Mixed Blood — and Mark Valdez — do all this work? It's more difficult to utilize the arts as a tool to increase a community's value than it is to merely put on a show, after all. In fact, the company's success as a social justice organization flies in the face of what most other companies around the country even *consider* doing. For too many, it would not even enter the mind of staff and board leaders of nonprofit arts organizations across America that a purpose could be anything but "putting on a great show."

The power of the arts is not limited to exuding beauty, providing an escape, or showcasing artistic skills. In fact, those aren't community powers at all. Any or all might be present within a particular artistic activity, but the value comes from the tangible, quantified positive impact the company has on the community ... just like any other kind of nonprofit.

Mark Valdez gets up in the morning to "serve my community and the greater society. That provides meaning for my life. Theater lets me serve; to do good." Shouldn't that be why every nonprofit arts organization exists? Isn't that more deserving of a seven-figure check than one that merely puts on a great show?

Seems to me that somebody should tell that to a major donor in Minnesota.

(With any luck, we just did.)

Just the Facts: Mixed Blood Theatre

Mission Statement

"Mixed Blood uses theater to disrupt injustice. We are a social justice organization catalyzing action and change through art. Our work is guided by deep community engagement and rooted in radical hospitality."

Tax Return

For the latest tax return, visit https://apps.irs.gov/app/eos/. Under "Search By," enter "Employer Identification Number (EIN)" and under "Search Term," enter 41-1377499. Or, you can always ask for a copy directly from the company. Please check the laws in your state and the state of Minnesota if you have questions.

Staff

Mark Valdez, Artistic Director
Alejandro Tey, Associate Artistic Director
Katy Vernon Underwood, Development Associate
Scott Edwards, Facility Director

Board of Directors *(as of August 2024)*
Joseph Stanley | President
Ken Rodgers | Vice President
Samantha King | Secretary
Kurt Gough | Treasurer

DJ Gramann II
Rodolfo Gutierrez
Daniel Le
Zoey Wainberg
Paul Whitaker
Mark Valdez

Winner of numerous awards for its human rights and artistic accomplishments, Mixed Blood celebrates differences and champions access. Mixed Blood achieves its mission through strategic programming at its own Alan Page Auditorium, within its Cedar Riverside neighborhood, and in off-site locations throughout the Twin Cities Metro area and the State of Minnesota.

Throughout its 48 years, Mixed Blood has been sustained by its adaptability and relationships. Programming has grown to include disability communities, immigrant and refugee populations, Minnesota Latinx, transgender and biracial Twin Citians, and the East African Muslims who reside in proximity to Mixed Blood's converted firehouse home.

Forklift Danceworks — Austin, Texas

The real people of Austin's Water Department in Forklift Danceworks' "The Way of Water" (Photo by Jonica Moore)

My favorite book about America is *Working* by Studs Terkel. In it, Terkel takes months to interview regular working people (and unemployed and retired people) in hundreds of jobs. They discuss what they do and what they get out of it. Their stories are familiar, unfamiliar, surprising, devastating, and hopeful. Truly an epic study on human nature and the ways in which Americans feel the freedom to be resilient, there is a pride of existence that even the most hopeless factory worker doing repetitive tasks can do.

A little over 50 years later, Mark Larson wrote an update on the book, *Working in the 21*st *Century,* which reports that Americans are a little less optimistic about the present and the future. Why wouldn't they be glum? In this portion of the life cycle that is described in great detail by Neil Howe and William Strauss in *The Fourth Turning,* a wintry pall has been cast over the prospects of those without ample cash, connections, and control.

Interview work, compilations of discussions into theater production or journalistic book-writing, has served America well. Beyond the entertainment value, which is keen, the process allows for the consumer (audience member, reader, etc.) to see that we are not so different, even though we are. Whether the work is controversial, such as Anna Deveare Smith's *Twilight: Los Angeles 1992,* in which over 200 interviews of people who were deeply affected by the riots following the verdict exonerating police officers who were caught collectively bullying and beating a prone Rodney King; or meant to catalyze a movement, such as Aaron Copeland's famous World War II clarion call, *Fanfare for the Common Man,* the celebration and uplifting of "regular" Americans dealing with serious issues has always appealed. Outrage begets outrage sometimes in the form of destructive violence, as often happens when a subjugated group of people treated inequitably. Smith's interviews and subsequent theatrical piece revealed a side of the participants and spectators that connected their psyches, humanizing the experience for everyone on all sides of the discussion and morphing outrage into action.

Turning outrage into action took place after Emily Mann's *Execution of Justice,* a stunning theatrical piece depicting the events surrounding the brutal act of violence in San Francisco when former Supervisor and police officer Dan White shot and killed Mayor George Moscone and Supervisor Harvey Milk, the first avowed homosexual to hold high public office in that city. After the trial, in which White blamed his actions on overstimulation caused by too many Twinkies, the defendant was convicted on the lesser charge of voluntary manslaughter. After serving a little more than five years, White took his own life. Mann's play caused spectators to evaluate their own feelings and forced them to act on the way in which the LGBT community on one side and the homophobes (using the original definition, the fear of homosexuality) on the other side have to face their own sense of humanity.

You may wonder what makes this kind of work fit within the structure of a 501(C)(3) arts organization. As always, return to the IRS itself when it defines tax-exempt activities. Included in the statute's exempt purposes are "lessening neighborhood tensions; eliminating prejudice and discrimination; [and] defending human and civil rights secured by law." Journalistically pure literary works such as *Working, Twilight: Los Angeles 1992, Execution of Justice*, and *Fanfare for the Common Man* are the kinds of documentary projects that make the case for a mission to connect people to gain understanding and tolerance — even with those that disagree with a point of view or way of life.

When audiences get a sample of humanity in the face of what could easily become cartoonish, one-dimensional depictions of certain moments in time, they naturally connect with each other and with their own inner feelings. When that happens, an intellectual analysis takes the place of raw fear and mindless protest and violence and people are given the chance to just be better next time. And "next time" is coming in a few years. It's as certain as continued climate chaos.

Ray Kurzweil's 2024 book *The Singularity Is Nearer* concluded that by the end of 2045, human beings and artificial intelligence will achieve something called "singularity." (If the hair on the back of your neck just went up, don't worry. You're not wrong about your fear.) "Singularity" can be described as the moment in which human and artificial intelligence will merge, a concept borrowed from the world of quantum physics. The upshot of that happenstance will likely lead to the elimination of most jobs from the workforce. Before we arrive there, we'll likely have just withstood a major war in America. The good news about that ("good" being a relative term) will be that following real war in this country — not wars propagated on foreign soil for others — Americans have often become comparatively self-sacrificing for the sake of the whole, at least temporarily, and at least for those who look like them.

As we celebrate the everyday workers in *Working*, we as audiences get a moment to step back and see the realities that face others. This is true charity: truly nonprofit purpose in action. In Austin, Texas, one company that specializes in spectacle dance works gives its participants the opportunity to change their own lives and to spread that change to others in their own community.

Welcome to **Forklift Danceworks.**

"We've got to figure out how to listen to each other and we've got to figure out how to hear each other's stories."

Those are the words of Allison Orr — erstwhile toddler teacher, potential Middle East negotiator, relationship expert, dancer, choreographer, cat-herder, problem-solver, distinguished fellow in Wesleyan's College of the Environment, and the founder and artistic director of Forklift Danceworks in Austin, Texas. Orr is not merely an impressive resume with a series of ivory tower ideas on how to make life better.

Allison Orr

"We have really big problems," bemoaned Orr. "Some of the most challenging issues humanity has ever faced. They're happening right now and I just can't waste my time with art that I don't feel addresses that, nor with people who don't want to. We don't have time to waste."

From sanitation workers to firefighters, power linemen to maintenance teams, Orr creates award-winning choreography with the people whose work sustains our everyday lives. Inspired by the beauty and virtuosity in the movement of labor, and building on her background in anthropology and social work, Allison has honed a methodology of ethnographic choreography that engages community members as co-authors and performers in the creation of large-scale civic spectacles. Challenging audiences to expand notions of dance and performer, her dances have been performed for audiences of 60 to more than 6,000.

For over 20 years, Forklift Danceworks has created inclusive, one-of-a-kind performance projects that share stories, build understanding, and create community. These works have reached over 50,000 people with free performances that typically feature the people whose work sustains our everyday lives. Additionally, Forklift Danceworks partners with different communities across the world to train local artists and government staff on the unique Forklift collaborative creative process. Through artistic programming and coaching, Forklift builds capacity for more informed civic dialogue, greater collaboration between individuals, and stronger connections and leadership across communities.

Past partners have included the City of Austin's Aquatics, Fire, Power, Sanitation, Urban Forestry and Watershed Protection Departments. The company has also partnered with Goodwill of Central Texas; Williams College Dining Services; Wake Forest University Facilities Services; and Wesleyan University Custodial, Grounds and Physical Plant teams. Internationally, the company has been commissioned by the Kyoto Arts Center and the International Community Arts Festivals, and it has created performances with the Japanese Women's Professional Baseball League in Kyoto, Japan, sanitation employees in Rotterdam and Barcelona, and Venetian gondoliers.

The education of artists and administrators continues to be a fly in the ointment of real progress in most nonprofit arts activity. Artists are trained in their art but not about their community – which is normal for jobbers whose careers navigate by piece or play (rather than a holistic look at a community's needs). Unfortunately, arts *administration* students are not trained about investigating a community's needs. Training starts and ends with the financial and physical operations of an organization and includes texts on how to raise funds, board composition, and maybe a sense of marketing. They may be trained to run an arts organization, but after the training is over and the student debt notices start to hit, they rarely have any idea as to why. Additionally, they are rarely asked to delve deeply into their own sense of curiosity to discover what will cause their art to improve the lives of the people in a community. Essentially, they are merely given examples of how flailing arts organizations currently run and are instructed to copy those practices.

As for artists, Orr believes their focus has been directed to be internal. If they are seeking to run a company, they're taught to have something called a "vision," with no connection between said vision and the reality of the community in which they live and work. "As artists, we're trained to think that we have to have a brilliant idea. After that happens, we're told that people will just follow us."

It's a crock.

The intent of Forklift is not "To inspire a lasting love and appreciation for dance through artistic excellence, exhilarating performances, innovative choreography, and superb educational programs," which is the corporately dismembered mission statement of the gargantuan Houston Ballet. That mission, along with so many others, is nothing more than an amalgam of subjective, meaningless, hyperbolic nonsense words, the purpose of which is to dodge their responsibility not only as a nonprofit, but as a company that means something to those outside its supercilious auspices.

"Our intent as an organization is not so different from my intent as its director," said Orr. "We want to activate communities. My intent and the intent of our work is to build and deepen connections and relationships between people who have not necessarily gathered together or worked together before. We build the muscle for collaboration, particularly in stakeholders that don't connect or cross. To solve our biggest challenges as a community, we need to know how to listen and collaborate, especially with people who we might not agree with."

When relationships are formed, deepened, challenged, and expanded among people who may disagree on their core values, the possibility for change becomes more likely. This kind of work from Forklift not only builds civic capacity, but social capital.

"I think a lot of our audience are interested Austinites who want to contribute to a better world, but quite don't know what that means," explained Orr. "So, they come to learn. We work a lot with frontline working-class personnel. I read that Studs Terkel once asked, 'When they were building the Great Wall of China, where did the masons go for lunch?' That's where the story is. Those are the people whose stories have to be told."

The general nature of a Forklift Danceworks event is by turns spectacular and homespun. One production in 2001 was *In Case of Fire,* Forklift's first collaboration with a City of Austin department. The piece featured thirteen Austin Firefighters, two fire engines, and a ladder truck. It was performed at the Austin Fire Department Training Tower and marked the culmination of Fire Prevention Week in Austin.

Orr worked with this group of firefighters for over a year — riding out on the trucks to fires and medical calls, interviewing the firefighters about their work, and learning all she could about firefighting. During the performance the firefighters were seen pulling hoses, climbing ladders, and rappelling down a building. Yes, there was fire.

Through choreography inspired by the movements that firefighters typically perform in their daily work, *In Case of Fire* showcased the important and often heroic work of City of Austin firefighters. When the dance came to a close the performing firefighters received a standing ovation from the audience of over 500 Austinites.

As Forklift's Krissie Marty wrote in a report published by the City of Austin, "The *My Park, My Pool, My City* project was a three-year artistic residency in partnership with the Parks and Recreation Department's Aquatics Division and several East Austin neighborhoods. Using three aquatic facilities in the Bartholomew, Dove Springs, and Givens neighborhoods as performance stages, the project activated and amplified civic engagement around the future of Austin's city pools. The community-based 'dances for city pools and their people' invited participation from Aquatics maintenance staff, lifeguards, pool users, and swimmers of all ages."

Administrative and municipal workers performing "My Park, My Pool, My City" at Austin's Dove Springs Pool (Photo by Jonica Moore)

"All the projects we design are based around the outcomes of our collaborators," said Orr. "We're currently working in Miami-Dade County with the Mayor's Office, Office of Resilience, and multiple city departments who engage with Miami-Dade's complex water issues. I've asked department leaders about their goals for our collaboration. What do they want to change in the way the public sees their work when the show is over? What could be different in Miami because of our work together?"

She continued. "We continually ask our stakeholders, our collaborators, and our partners: to what should we be held accountable? What would success look like to you? That guides me in the content creation. So the content of the projects really comes from the people who are in the shows and the people who are the partnering to make it happen with us."

But the work doesn't stop there.

Allison Orr (L) and the "dancers" in Forklift Danceworks's "Way of Water: Onion Creek" (Photo by Jonica Moore)

"Then we survey audience members. After we get the results, we follow up with all the collaborators who were part of the project. These are the employees who perform, the supervisors who consulted — the leadership of the departments. We go back and we collect their feedback. We ask questions such as, 'Did the project improve morale? Do your employees think of themselves as more creative? Did Forklift bring value to your department? Did the project strengthen communication in your organization?' And then, I'll sit down and interview key people, sometimes on camera, to get feedback and impact. Lynn Osgood, who did our research around our three-year residency with Austin aquatics, looked at individual impact, workforce impact, neighborhood impact, and citywide impact. Lynn noted that during our project, Austin voters approved the largest bond ever in the history of the city for aquatics. A budget officer also came to one of our shows, and his visit turned into action. $1.5 million annually was added to the Aquatics budget. Not every project leads to these kinds of dramatic economic benefits, but these were exciting outcomes."

Orr talked often about the fact that once she chose to establish a nonprofit, the art could no longer be just for her.

"We just asked the Lower Colorado River Authority (LCRA) if we could help them with their needs. The LCRA is the non-governmental entity in Texas that manages our portion of the Colorado River. I see a dance on a dam, but that doesn't mean that might be the best dance to help them with their communication needs. That's also what makes it different for me and Forklift. We have to address our partners' return on investment from the very beginning. Even with a 20+ year track record of success with all sorts of governmental and regional agencies, I still have to be clear about what's in it for our partners, not for me and Forklift."

Too many artists running too many nonprofit arts organizations never put that thought into their brain, even though that's the core of what nonprofits are supposed to do.

Given her background, which also includes studies in cultural anthropology, social work, pre-school education, and whatever else piqued her bottomless sense of curiosity, Allison Orr will always be mid-sentence, mid-career, and in the middle of everything.

"I'm the luckiest person," she crowed. "I got to ride on the back of a firetruck for a year. I rode on the back of a trash truck. I hung out with transmission linemen who free-climb 250 feet high. I have the best life. What it all boils down to is this: I love culture. I love stories. I love being with people, just in regular life, and I'm a little bit on a mission to get art at the center of how we solve problems. In my soul, I feel really like we need this tool. As a people, we have to figure out how to listen to each other and we have to figure out how to hear each other's stories."

Orr's husband, kids, the rest of her family, and her company people know her passions.

"Forklift is a family project. Mine came with me to Japan. They've come with me to Connecticut. Now my children know sanitation workers. They know linemen. They know our city's pool whisperers. All of our lives are bigger because of this work. But you know what? I'm the one who's gotten the most out of it. I really am. I really don't feel like I'm here to save anybody. That's not the point. But all the relationships and connections … *That's* why I get up in the morning."

She talked about once wanting to be a Middle East peace negotiator. With her drive, energy, and data that shows the detail of how art can prove to be an effect tool for growing relationships among disparate people, it would not surprise me to see Forklift do a production at the United Nations featuring diplomatic attachés from warring factions in a choreographed exposition of peacemaking duties, and in doing so, ending all tensions among people who hold no trust whatsoever for the other.

If you're interested, give Allison Orr a call. But if you're *really* interested in attaining peace, send Forklift a seven-figure check tomorrow, writing this note on the memo line: "If anyone can do it, you can."

Just the Facts: Forklift Danceworks

Mission Statement

"Forklift Danceworks activates communities through a collaborative, creative process."

Tax Return

For the latest tax return, visit https://apps.irs.gov/app/eos/. Under "Search By," enter "Employer Identification Number (EIN)" and under "Search Term," enter 01-0812720. Or, you can always ask for a copy directly from the company. Please check the laws in your state and the state of Texas if you have questions.

Staff

Allison Orr, Founder and Artistic Director
Krissie Marty, Associate Artistic Director & Community Collaborations Director
Lisa Byrd, Operational Strategist
Francis Rodriguez, Choreographer & Program Coordinator
Qainta Harris, Director of Development & Communications
Rachael Garbowski, Associate Director of Development & Communications
Jennifer Berrong, Development & Communications Manager
Marina Garbalena, Development & Communications Associate
Emily Morgan, Research Fellow
Damian Flores, Digital Media Coordinator

Board of Directors ***(as of August 2024)***
Alejandra Hamlet, President
Ezequiel Calderon, Jr., Vice-President
Adriana Graf, Treasurer
Don Baylor, Secretary

Cybill Guess
Cecilia Camarillo
Kate Donaho
Sarah Finley
Samuel Gilbert
Gaurav Jain
Cari Marshall
Ashley McLain
Ayleen J. Pérez
Lizette Resendez
Jeff Trucksess

> *Forklift Danceworks is completely revamping creative expression by fusing artistic dance with local and global initiatives. Their latest production, The Way of Water, explores the human experience with water and focuses on those who steward it. This multi-year global performance will occur in four cities: Austin, El Paso, Miami, and Venice, Italy. Forklift kicked off The Way of Water: Onion Creek, choosing to focus on the Onion Creek watershed because of frequent flooding. With the help of the Austin Watershed Protection Department, Forklift uplifts the Watershed Protection staff and local youth through lively performances that incorporate job movements.*
>
> *— EASTside Magazine, Austin*

Arts Capacity – Chicago, Illinois

One of the great bugaboos of the nonprofit industry is that, while it must be responsive and responsible to the communities in which each individual charity operates, the definition of community can sometimes be purposely made vague to suit the organization's operations.

Nonprofit *arts* organizations that continue to portray themselves as art-for-art's-sake entities that reap giant donations from wealthy people serving their own needs have little concept of community. They tend to equate "community" with "audience" as though no other entity were important enough to serve. It's a perverse definition, of course, in the true definition of perverse – "per-verse (pər-vərs ′), *adj*. Showing a deliberate and obstinate desire to behave in a way that is unreasonable or unacceptable, often in spite of the consequences."

A community to be served cannot be defined solely in terms of ticket-buyers and donors. That kind of self-indulgent, wrongheaded thinking in the nonprofit arts sector has relegated it to the irrelevant elitist dog show that it has become.

Some organizations, such as the Louisville Orchestra and Out of Hand, have chosen to define their communities by geography and need. Need is the primary characteristic of a community in terms of charitable work, not an affinity to art.

However, a community is defined as a group of people whose relationship to each other defines their existence. One nonprofit arts organization defines it like few others.

Welcome to **Arts Capacity.**

"I think it's the structure in our country that doesn't allow us to be our best selves," said Arts Capacity's founder, Holly Mulcahy, a brilliant orchestral musician in her own right. "We're considered elitist, and it just boils down to human nature, wanting to belong and wanting to exclude. To me, that defeats the purpose of what we have. It's wanting to feel like you're part of something, and in order to do that, you need to exclude somebody else. The classical arts have never gotten away from that structure that started in Europe, where our patrons were kings and where artists were at the mercy of the wealthy."

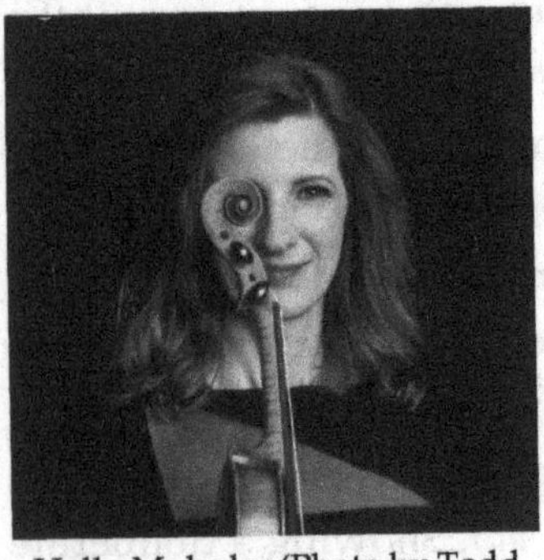
Holly Mulcahy (Photo by Todd Rosenberg)

If not for Arts Capacity, an organization created to pull together and solve the problems of the incarcerated community — and yes, that *is* a community — the general public and the prisoners themselves would be relegated to an unrelenting vicious cycle of crime, incarceration, release, quick recidivism, incarceration, quick recidivism, etc.

They do not work with the incarcerated community in order to get good reviews, achieve some vague definition of excellence, or to sell albums. The company's intention is to create a better world. The core of the mission statement can be restated as this: "Arts Capacity helps people in need." As their website states, they do it through establishing a common language of music in order to help prisoners "cope with challenges and develop the capacity to experience change for good."

"Our intent is twofold," continued Mulcahy. "We offer a way for the incarcerated population to use music and the arts to find feelings, to harness ways to connect with people through prosocial behaviors, to enhance emotional intelligence, all using a platform of either creating art or digesting art. The other reason is that I wanted to quantify the value of music. In this industry — whether it's symphonic, chamber, or what have you — we all say 'Music makes you feel better. It's so wonderful. It's so good for you.' But we don't quantify it. That's what I've been doing for eight years, is gathering the data. I can give you the numbers, and I can give you the success rates to quantify the value of the arts."

"In the symphony world," she sighed, "where I have been for 30 years, everybody is convinced that children need music. Children need concerts. 'We must have busloads of kids coming to our concert halls.' Then the only data that some organizations show is that 30,000 kids come to their concerts. But that's not a metric, is it? If nothing else happens, it's just a pleasant field trip. Arts Capacity does keep quantifying. Sure, we know how many people show up. But we also know if the audience is growing, what kind of music they like, how they like the music, how it's tracking, and how it's affecting recidivism. It's taken eight years to get the recidivism data metric."

"Some of the surprises come with new looks at the data," she beamed. "How is what we do positively impacting prison staff? How is it positively impacting the regular concert audiences that are curious. Why did a given prisoner resonate with a Jennifer Higdon string trio, and why should I go to live music concerts? That anecdotal data is important stuff, and we can point exactly to why that conversation got started. So it's not just prisons, it's 360 degrees, expanded in every direction."

Arts Capacity's devotion to service came, at least at first, without the ropes of extortion that too often accompany major gifts. Mulcahy was the concertmaster for the Chattanooga Symphony Orchestra and started this program 30 miles south of there, at Walker State Prison in Georgia.

"Of course, we had to meet budget and to pay musicians," Mulcahy recollected. "But it wasn't like we need a gigantic chunk of cash. We started with a story. We started to show the success rate of prisoners. It was the focus on impact that manifested amazing curiosity from donors big and small. We focus on the story of why music works for this population and how it can work for anybody on the outside who may have life struggles that are similar to, say, Inmate John Doe at Walker. We came out with sincere, heartfelt stories. We've shared those just here and there on social media for the last eight years, that started to draw attention, and the attention started to get exponentially larger. Then when we felt it was right, when we could stand on our own and say, you know, we've done this the right way, which is we're it's not about us, it's about what the music does. The centerpiece of this is what music does for people. We're standing on proof, and we're standing on something that has been sincere from the get-go. I'm just, I'm totally in love with all of this, because it speaks so much to why nonprofit arts organizations exist."

As stated in this book and the previous editions of the *Scene Change* series, a lot of arts organization leaders wear blinders so that they don't have to see poor or needy people, let alone help them. They complain when asked to do so. "That's not what we do," as though that's a valid excuse for eschewing their responsibilities as a nonprofit organization. Arts Capacity, on the other hand, shows the public that it is, in fact, sympathetic to the negative issues facing the total community – and specifically, to the incarcerated community.

"It's easy to go play in a hospital for kids," lamented Mulcahy. "That's expected in our society, because those are good people. They're victims, they're heroes. Well, I'm playing for people who might have committed a crime against you. These people each had a story that started with making a bad choice. Maybe they grew up with nothing but bad choices. But if music is a universal good, I wanted to see if I could quantify that good for these people."

She continued enthusiastically. "How can music help people find their own emotions, temper their own emotions. How can it help their own creativity? How can it help them connect with their families? It's never been about saving people. I'm not here to offer music because, 'you poor thing, you need it.' From that, we discovered that the stories that people have in these situations mirror society in uncomfortable but awesome ways. That discovery helped me amplify what I do on stage for the paying audience."

I asked her for her definition of a prison community. The depth of the answer surprised me.

"Every single prison has a different culture. For instance, the Walker State Prison, which is a medium-security, faith- and character-based prison, is fully supported by the community. They've got church support, they have job support, they've got college classes. They have high school GED. They are supported. It's a healthy culture for a prison.

"Some of the prisons in Kansas have large populations. They are not faith and character based. Their populations are maximum- and Supermax-security, which means that they include the worst crimes. There are lifers in there. It's equally important to give the lifers the same kind of care and treatment as the people who are going to get out. Lifers are pillars. If you mistreat the lifers, they're going to treat everybody around them badly, including the new prisoners that come in. If you treat a lifer well and with respect, they're going to set the tone. They know they're never getting out. But they're going to set the tone and be supportive of the people that will."

The lifers are the community's elders.

[Arts Capacity] has made me think of the music I listen to, and how sometimes it puts me in a bad mood, but this music makes me want to listen to better music so my moods will be better. Thank you for this day.

— Inmate, Hutchinson Correctional Facility, Hutchinson, Kansas

---

"Here's why the lifers are important," said Mulcahy. "You're talking about somebody that's going to be spending time in a prison, maybe 50, 60, 70, years, depending on when they enter, they're never getting out. But think how many wardens they're going to see. Think of how many staff changes they're going to see. The workers are not pillars. Those are people that are going to a job. But the people who are stuck in the prison are so much more important as far as keeping the culture positive, and a warden can make it or break it for those people, especially for the other part of the community: their children, their families, The wives, the friends on the outside — these are the people that we don't talk about in society. Prisoners might be seen as just people to be warehoused and forgotten about. But people like you and me — we might have somebody in prison to go visit. We might be children that go to visit their parents. So it's important to make sure those communications are stable and open and available. There's a lot of stigma, but the part of the community that is outside of the prison is very much attached."

Outside the prison walls, performances and workshops can bring families together. Arts Capacity produced an opera for the inmates of Walker State Prison. After that, at the request of the prisoners themselves, they did a second performance outside the walls. That legitimized the art that was created. They performed the same piece for the prison families at no cost.

This was a stunningly happy discovery for Mulcahy.

"Many times," she said, "prisoners will take our concert programs and mail them to their children, and their children will start the clarinet, or the children will start the violin, and that gives them something to talk about at visitation. Both the prisoners and their children talk about music."

In the summer of 2024, Mulcahy and the group performed at a Level Four and Five prison in brutally hot Arizona. One of the inmates regularly downloads opera. Pardon the expression, but he's a die-hard opera fan now.

She has listened both to supporters and detractors of the program. The latter group generally believes that prisoners should not receive any services. To them, the words "Correctional Facility" are just that, words. They believe prison should be all about punishment and not at all about rehabilitation or attempting to remove recidivism from the equation. Mulcahy has an answer to that group of individuals.

"Like it or not, the people who get out will be your future neighbors," she tells them. "Do you want them to be able to handle their emotions because they've discovered new ways to process that through music? Or do you want them to come out just knowing how to weld and not process emotions? Asking those questions to people takes the defensive mechanism out."

These are the laws. Any judgment short of the death penalty tells us that the corrections system should be in the business of correcting, not punishing. But Mulcahy and Arts Capacity are not looking at the population through rose-colored glasses.

"They've committed terrible crimes," said Mulcahy, "but I wasn't in their shoes when they committed them. I didn't grow up the way they did. You just don't know. But what I do know is the people that are going to get out are terrified. They're embarrassed. They don't know what to expect, and if they are supported well, as they are at Walker State Prison, there's a better chance for winning. Don't we all want that in our society, a better chance for winning?

"When they get out, should they continue to be punished? The law says no. I'm not a lawyer, but I know that when they get out, there's a certain process. When that stops, they're out, they're done. They've paid their price. But still, some of them can't vote. Some cannot get jobs, because, you know, you check that box on the job application, and that's it. So what are these people supposed to do? They're still here. Don't we want them to be a functioning part of society, right?"

Conscience has a large role in the purpose of Arts Capacity. It's at a higher level than "there but for the grace," which leans more toward sympathy or empathy. Conscience makes it impossible for Mulcahy *not* to help this forgotten community.

"I've put hundreds of thousands of dollars into myself, into my instrument, my time, and sitting up on stage. When I look at an orchestra cutting budgets, cutting musicians, and you're not blind — you can actually see that the audience is shrinking — it's natural to wonder, 'Why did I do this? Why bother?' That's at the root of Arts Capacity. It's like watering a plant that's dry. If you can, why wouldn't you?"

It's an incredibly gifted, passionate, and supportive team at Arts Capacity. The board, the employees, the volunteers, all embrace the "Yes, and..." principles of improvisation. They make things happen even without the immediate knowledge of the source of funding.

"When times get tough, our industry tends to exclude the heck out of ourselves," said Mulcahy. "But when you bring people into the process — the creative process, the collaborative process — and ask 'Do you want in?' Then your company has power. When you're losing money and you start to close in and try to consolidate all the decisions so that they come from just a few chosen folks, your company loses that power. That's what we do. We open it up instead of close it down."

As I do with every company leader, I asked Mulcahy to tell me (without using the words in the mission statement) her description of the punch-to-the-gut mission.

"It's music for the people and people matter, making the music matter."

Why does the music matter?

"It's a platform for community, and many times when there's miscommunications in our screwed up and challenging world, music and the arts allow for a way to speak to each other in new ways that are productive in expressing our human condition."

Just the Facts: Arts Capacity

Mission Statement

"Arts Capacity helps people in need through the power of art, culture, communication, and live music to cope with challenges and develop the capacity to experience change for good."

Tax Return

For the latest tax return, visit https://apps.irs.gov/app/eos/. Under "Search By," enter "Employer Identification Number (EIN)" and under "Search Term," enter 82-1796413. Or, you can always ask for a copy directly from the company. Please check the laws in your state and the state of Illinois if you have questions.

Staff

Holly Mulcahy, Executive and Artistic Director

Board of Directors ***(as of August 2024)***

Tyler Rand, President

Tim Hinck, Vice-President

Dr. Steve Hawkins, Treasurer

Barbara Scowcroft, Secretary
Alan Bonderud
Jeremy Stroop
Kelly Stultz
Jack Wilds

As incarcerated people prepare for reentry into society, they are given tools. These tools sometimes include training in a trade or learning how to succeed in job interviews. But often, the most important tools are overlooked in preparing people's return to society. With Arts Capacity, my vision is to share tools that allow people to access their own emotions, creativity, and humanity that will empower them and help them succeed as free citizens. By sharing music and culture, the goal to help people find a coping mechanism or emotional outlet is a powerful way to re-humanize a population that will eventually be our future neighbors.

— Holly Mulcahy

Epilogue

First, a pre-epilogue.

There were several more nonprofit arts organizations that get it. They deserve recognition and funding as well, even if they didn't happen to make it into the *Scene Change* series. I recommend you take a look at **Cornerstone Theater Company** of Los Angeles, which has been profiled on television magazines, print media and more. Much like Forklift Danceworks, their mission is to "collaborate with communities," not for their art, but for the communities' well-being.

I'd also recommend a visit to **Mural Arts Philadelphia**, which believes that "art ignites change"; **Youth Speaks** of San Francisco, whose mission is to "challenge youth to develop and amplify their voices as creators of societal change"; **The International Wow Company** of New York, which "is a film, theater, and civic engagement company made up of filmmakers, theater-makers, writers, activists, actors, and artists from diverse cultural backgrounds.... The company was founded to create new socially conscious work and also, importantly, to engage with its audience to foster activism and participation in the political process. who collaborate to create new work that addresses current international social, environmental, and political crises"; and the promise borne by the once-venerable, now-enthusiastically community-centered **Long Wharf Theatre** in Connecticut, which made the radical decision to upend the caste system ordained by its own past and re-invent themselves by transitioning out of its longtime home on Sargent Drive in New Haven, Connecticut, to staging shows in various venues around the city *specifically for the people of New Haven.*

Near my home in greater Seattle is **Key to Change**, led by internationally renowned violinist Quinton Morris, and whose mission is to make "world-class music instruction accessible to young people from underserved communities." A note (no pun intended) on Quinton Morris and Key to Change: the mission statement is modest in comparison to their impact. They use music instruction to build confidence and grow the capacity of kids living in desperate circumstances, they don't charge for the process (they really depend on donations to buy all those violins and violas they distribute), and from a small seed of interest, they've blossomed into the leading impact nonprofit among all the arts nonprofits in the region.

You should send Key to Change a check, too. In fact, send a monthly donation.

Books can only be so long, which is why all these wonderful companies did not make it. But they're all doing better work than their brethren among the largest organizations in their respective regions, who want more money, more money, more money, and provide little impact to the community at large. And before you choke on that truth, remember this: *the mere production of art — any art, regardless of whether it's "excellent" or "horse-hockey" — is not a tax-exempt activity, according to the only source that matters, the Internal Revenue Service.* There's a reason for that.

Art, by itself, is essential, but arts organizations are not. It is incumbent on all of us to support those companies that are not pretending to be charitable organizations by flouting a 501(C)(3) letter from the IRS as proof of worth. The court system allowed arts organizations to become nonprofit, but the public has spoken on the subject of the general essential nature of nonprofit arts organizations. They have roundly, loudly, emphatically pulled their support. That support, as evidenced by the companies in this book, can only return when these organizations stop acting like money-grubbing behemoths bullying donations out of unwitting (and often toxic) donors – including foundation and government leaders, who should know better – and find ways to prove charitable impact. Just like every other kind of nonprofit organization in America. Until an entire generation of nonprofit artistic directors, executive directors, managing directors, and board members die off (much like their Methuselah-like donors themselves), the best we can do is use whatever power we have as lovers of art to promote the best of the best impactors with our voices, our donations, and our time. This book represents a road map to that effort.

Okay, now the real epilogue.

I don't hate the arts. I love the arts so much that it pains me that funding has evaporated. It pains me that the nonprofit organizations themselves have allowed that to happen, often for the sake of some artistic vainglory. It perplexes me that there are leaders who *still* believe funding will magically return. It riles me that new arts organizations receive their nonprofit letter and try to use it as a basis for worth, when really, it's just a piece of paper that is a basis for existence and nothing more. It really pisses me off that leaders who know better continue to toady up to toxic donors who want to use their donation not for any grand purpose for the organization, but for the purpose of showing elite status.

On the one hand, arts organizational funding is disappearing. If you're reading the lines themselves (no need to read between them), I'm advocating for organizations to stop scrounging for money from supercilious clods. So where is the money to be had?

If these are the thoughts running through your brain, you've been brainwashed to think that arts organizations deserve money because, well, they're arts organizations. You've been brainwashed to think about funding more than thinking about your community. Nonprofit organizations, in general, provide impact, and when they provide a lot of it, they raise a lot of money. Simple as that.

So what do you do next? Go bankrupt?

Oddly, for some companies, that's probably not a bad idea. A soulless, impact-bereft, non-community-centric organization that closes is better than one that vacuums money out of the arts-mosphere to fund a seventh development person, a ninth actor, or a new, state-of-the-art stage turntable.

But for most, you're simply going to have to have a come-to-Jesus meeting with your leading stakeholders. You're going to have to allow all the players, from the artists to the staff to the ushers to the C-Suite to the members of the Board, to be able to mold the company into not merely an artistic force for beauty and provocation of thought, but into one that joyfully practices its responsibility to quantifiably help the people who live there.

Like the Louisville Orchestra, the best arts organizations are those that cannot, will not, and *don't want to* exist somewhere else. They're looking for people in their own sphere of influence — like that girl whose life was saved because she found music that was introduced by the LO — to positively affect in ways that make them better citizens, more tolerant people, and able to confront the problems within their society effectively. If the arts organization that has your heart follows someone's artistic vision over all else, then there's no reason it needs to exist as a nonprofit. Nonprofits help the people in their own communities. Ask yourself: how does my arts nonprofit do that? And why?

Not every organization, as I've said before, needs to close down. It might be that there is no desire from any stakeholder to help anyone. If their only desire is to produce "excellent" art ("excellent" is in quotations because it's a totally subjective term), that's okay. Just take the next step and convert the company into a profit-making company. Instead of donors, acquire investors (and pay them some sort of dividend or other ROI). Form a Limited Liability Corporation (LLC) instead of a 501(C)(3) corporation. Or even, if you prefer, a Low-Profit Limited Liability Corporation (L3C). Talk to a CPA about all those options.

Then, convert your artistic department into a research and development team. Turn your development staff into financial managers and salespeople, working with a newly focused marketing team for the sole purpose of attracting funds.

Look, there is no moral high ground to being a nonprofit. Entrepreneurial activity can be extraordinarily fulfilling and financial engines for a region without having to register as a charity.

Charities are hard. Their worth is measured in impact, not in financial profit and loss. As business guru and bestselling author Jim Collins wrote in his monograph, *Good to Great and the Social Sectors* (Collins preferred the term "social sectors" to "nonprofits"):

> We must reject the idea—well-intentioned, but dead wrong—that the primary path to greatness in the social sectors is to become "more like a business." Most businesses—like most of anything else in life—fall somewhere between mediocre and good. Few are

> great. When you compare great companies with good ones, many widely practiced business norms turn out to correlate with mediocrity, not greatness. So, then, why would we want to import the practices of mediocrity into the social sectors? That's when it dawned on me: we need a new language. The critical distinction is not between business and social, but between great and good. We need to reject the imposition of the 'language of business' in the social sectors, and instead jointly embrace a language of greatness.

Your community does not have the time, the money, or the inclination to support nonprofit organizations that do not choose to be great. They've proven that by pulling funding away from nonprofit arts organizations in particular, mostly because they believe that these organizations only really care about their wealthy donors and ticket buyers, also known as their "audience."

Choose to be great, not by pursuing some undefinable notion of excellence. Choose to be great, not by exploiting the children who pay for classes at your last gala. Choose to be great, not by wasting countless millions of dollars on a new building for some lasting legacy of the wealthiest donor whose name is on the front archway. Choose to be great, not by buddying up with the most toxic people in your community who just want the company to revolve around their needs.

No.

Choose to be great by pursuing a community that is materially better off because of the work you do to help them.

That's when your organization will matter. The companies in this book all did that. Now it's your turn.

Lastly, as you may have expected, a post-epilogue:

The good news is right there in front of you. The current winter of our nonprofit arts organizational discontent is not immutable nor lethal, but only when you think of your community's needs before your own. Financing change is difficult, but it has been done plenty of times. All you need is want-to and an idea of how and why the human beings (especially those who are underserved or totally unserved) in your community deserve to be better off than they are now.

For-profit businesses can lose money for years and still (ultimately) succeed if they find a way to adapt. Why? Because they have access to funding that nonprofits don't have: venture capital.

Nonprofits don't get venture capital – especially nonprofit arts organizations.

Why not? Tradition. Bad press. Overly restrictive "best" practices.

The public has been taught (incorrectly) that nonprofits and their employees must scrape by, no matter what. They're pilloried if they want to run a deficit budget in order to invest in anything. Nonprofits, especially arts organizations, are only allowed to raise enough money every year to do the work they do in that particular year.

Sometimes, there are multi-year pledges or gifts. But even so, they are usually not designed for making the nonprofit arts organization more impactful to their communities. Too often, they're for multi-year discrete projects meant to increase artistic excellence. Or, as one ex-monk did after winning a $250 million lottery, the money is given to allow artistic directors to do ambitious work that they've always wanted to do, regardless of the impact of the citizenry of the region in which the money was given.

Sorry, padre, it ain't about the art, it's about the people.

The only way in which your nonprofit is allowed to get venture capital, when you ask around, is through a throat-strangling endowment fund that rolls off a whopping 3–5% of its value to your nonprofit's budget each year. As a Ford

Foundation finance specialist once told me, "If you're not rolling off 20% of your annual budget from your endowment, you shouldn't really have an endowment."

As a result, when nonprofit arts leaders do long-range planning of any kind, they think in terms of survival instead of thriving. They have no financial incentive to change course when necessary. When they do change course, they have to expend a great deal of personal capital and psychic energy to gather buy-in from all the other stakeholders. Meanwhile, they have to run the current version of the arts organization, even when they know that their future is doomed.

They are forced to fix the plane while flying it. Even if the plane is breaking down. Even if it's going in the wrong direction.

Stop. If you run an arts organization that is flailing because it refuses to act as a charity, and has become an obsolete, elitist vestige of some sort of golden time 50 years ago (that likely never occurred), you have to find a way to stop. It's not the best way to go, but if you can't raise venture capital to cover the initial losses of the new, impactful version of your arts organization, that's the last arrow in your quiver.

Stop. You handicap yourself by trying to continue an old, unworkable model of "art for art's sake" and tweaking it to gain popularity as your sole goal.

Stop. Especially when you already know that change is not only necessary, it's the only path to sustainability.

Stop. Land. Let the current passengers deplane. Look at the plane and marvel at the fact that no one died while riding in it.

Start. Initiate the conversations with your community leaders about what they feel are the most important needs, how you can help solve or mitigate them with your arts organization, and why your company is best placed to do those kinds of indispensable activities.

Start. Find ways within your own connections to get some venture capital (or the equivalent), not for a one-off artistic venture, but for a holistic positive approach to improving the lives of the people of your community. Find the financing to run a big ol' deficit budget for a year if you have to (there's no law that says that you have to present a break-even budget every year). That's the kind of investment instrument that keeps entrepreneurial companies going.

Change. Transform the dynamic of donations not as play sponsorships, but as task sponsorships that span the lifetime of the organization (and not for the engagement of a play, exhibit, or other artistic venture).

The wage gap, wealth gap, and trust gap is increasing, even though we're more aware that inequity exists than ever before. Is this why so many young people are eschewing their dreams of a better world through the arts? Is this why there's a nonprofit skills gap even though thousands graduate from arts management programs each year, taking with them the kind of debt load that wages from a nonprofit arts organization cannot currently help pay off? Is that why those same students, people who have a passion for the arts, are leaving their chosen field to go work for whatever tech company will pay them the most?

In four words, yes.

Have the courage to stop the current inessential nonprofit arts organization model. You can do it. Be willing to create a new, viable path for your community's success. You can do that, too. All you have to do is land the plane.

It makes sense to stop what you're doing and start fresh. Maybe, without the extraneous noise, the core of your leadership can figure out a way to become the essential business most nonprofit organizations claim to be (but aren't). Or maybe, if they can't (or rather, won't), maybe it's time to create the kind of vacuum that nature abhors. If you don't choose to be indispensable to your community's stated needs, maybe another visionary arts organization already does, and they deserve all the support in the world.

Then, take off. Soar. Glory in the knowledge that people are made better by what you do. It's the greatest glory there is.

Now, put the book down for the moment, tell ten friends in the business to pick up copies of the *Scene Change* series, and get started. I'm genuinely excited for you. It's going to be great.

Related Media

Harrison, Alan. Scene Change: Why Today's Nonprofit Arts Organizations Have to Stop Producing Art and Start Producing Impact. Changemakers Books, 2024. Duh.

Harrison, Alan. Scene Change 2: The Five **Real** Responsibilities of Nonprofit Boards. Changemakers Books, 2024. Double-duh.

Abrams, Teddy, and Michael Tilson Thomas. The American Project (recording). Yuja Wang, soloist, with the Louisville Orchestra. Deutsche Grammaphon. Released 2023.

Borwick, Doug. Engage Now! A Guide to Making the Arts Indispensable. ArtsEngaged, 2015.

Collins, Jim. Good to Great and the Social Sectors. Harper Business, 2005

Kurzweil, Ray. The Singularity Is Nearer: When We Merge with AI. Viking, 2024.

Larson, Mark. Working in the 21st Century: An Oral History of American Work in a Time of Social and Economic Transformation. Midway Books/Agate Publishing, 2024

Mann, Emily. Execution of Justice. Samuel French, 1985.

Orr, Allison. Danceworks: Stories of Creative Collaboration. Wesleyan University Press, 2023.

Sims-Alvarado, Karcheik. Atlanta and the Civil Rights Movement: 1944–1968 (Images of America). Arcadia Publishing, 2017.

Smith, Anna Deveare. Twilight: Los Angeles, 1992. Knopf-Doubleday Publishing Group, 1994.

Strauss, William, and Neil Howe. The Fourth Turning: An American Prophecy. Broadway Books, 1998.

Terkel, Studs. Working: People Talk About What They Do All Day and How They Feel About What They Do. Pantheon, 1974.

Wallace, Christina, Henry W. McGee, Rohit Deshpande, and Max Hancock. Out of Hand Theater: Monetizing Creativity. Harvard Business Review. March 15, 2024.

Wooden, John R., and Steve Jamison. Wooden: A Lifetime of Observations and Reflections On and Off the Court. Contemporary Books, 1997.

About Alan Harrison FRSA

Alan Harrison FRSA is the author of *Scene Change: Why Today's Nonprofit Arts Organizations Have to Stop Producing Art and Start Producing Impact* and *Scene Change 2: The Five REAL Responsibilities for a Nonprofit Arts Board.* He is and has been a father, writer, stage and film actor, nonprofit executive, cabaret piano player (but not a good one), composer, playwright, singer, columnist, critic, voice actor, association executive, and an arts-related board president (in no particular order). Recently, he was inducted as a Fellow into London's Royal Society for Arts, hence the four capital letters that follow his last name.

(I know. I was surprised, too.)

For the past 30 years, he has led, produced, directed, promoted, raised money for, succeeded, and failed in over 300 theatrical productions on Broadway and off and at prestigious (and not-so-prestigious) nonprofit arts organizations across the United States. Among those organizations were Lincoln

Center Theater, the Los Angeles Theatre Center, The Pasadena Playhouse, Pittsburgh Public Theater, Seattle Repertory Theatre, the Alabama Shakespeare Festival, and ArtsWest.

Along with writing books, Alan speaks to various arts-specific audiences on the power of choosing to become a charitable organization that happens to use art as a tool. He has spoken at conferences, on podcasts, and in boardrooms about the positive power people in the business have to save the nonprofit arts industry from itself.

He has a terrific son, Danny Harrison, and a partner in crime, Donna Oslin, who keep him in check … and stitches.

Oh, right. He's also a two-time *Jeopardy!* champion so, you know, there's that.

A Special Note to You, the Reader

Thank you for purchasing *Scene Change 3*. I hope you've also picked up a copy of the first and second books in the series, and can now be comfortable in using these stories and companies to further your own goals as a twenty-first-century nonprofit arts leader, one that leans more on the "nonprofit" than the "arts." My sincere hope is that you derived as much from reading this book as I have in creating it.

If you have a few moments, please feel free to add your review of the book at your favorite online site for feedback. It helps to get the message out about the future of nonprofit arts organizations and for some reason, folks seem to care about 5-star reviews enough to want to read the material.

Please visit my website for news, recent blog posts, and to sign up for my newsletter: **https://501c3.guru**. On the site, you'll find easy ways to contact me about the issues you might be facing within your own nonprofit arts organization. If you need help, please contact me by email, phone, or LinkedIn. I'd be delighted to chat.

Sincerely,

Current Bestsellers from Changemakers Books

Resetting Our Future: Am I Too Old to Save the Planet? A Boomer's Guide to Climate Action
Lawrence MacDonald

Why American boomers are uniquely responsible for the climate crisis — and what to do about it.

Resetting Our Future: Feeding Each Other Shaping Change in Food Systems through Relationship
Michelle Auerbach and Nicole Civita

Our collective survival depends on making food systems more relational; this guidebook for shaping change in food systems offers a way to find both security and pleasure in a more connected, well-nourished life.

Resetting Our Future: Zero Waste Living, The 80/20 Way The Busy Person's Guide to a Lighter Footprint
Stephanie J. Miller

Empowering the busy individual to do the easy things that have a real impact on the climate and waste crises.

The Way of the Rabbit
Mark Hawthorne

An immersion in the world of rabbits: their habitats, evolution and biology; their role in legend, literature, and popular culture; and their significance as household companions.